Substance Abuse
and Family Therapy

Family Therapy
Theory, Practice, and Technique

Vincent D. Foley, Ph.D.   SERIES EDITOR

Also in this series

Structural Family Therapy   Carter C. Umbarger, Ph.D.

Substance Abuse and Family Therapy

Edward Kaufman, M.D.
Associate Professor
California College of Medicine
Department of Psychiatry and Human Behavior

Director of Psychiatric Education
Director of Family Therapy Training
University of California
Irvine, California

GRUNE & STRATTON, INC.
(*Harcourt Brace Jovanovich, Publishers*)

Orlando   San Diego   New York
London   Toronto   Montreal   Sydney   Tokyo

Library of Congress Cataloging in Publication Data

Kaufman, Edward.
  Substance abuse and family therapy.

  Includes bibliographies and index.
  1. Substance abuse. 2. Family psychotherapy. I. Title.
[DNLM: 1. Family Therapy. 2. Substance Abuse—therapy.
WM 270 K21s]
RC564.K38   1984   616.86   84-12891
ISBN 0-8089-1679-3

Grune & Stratton, Inc.
Orlando, Florida, 32887

Distributed in the United Kingdom by
Grune & Stratton, Ltd.
24/28 Oval Road, London NW 1

Library of Congress Catalog Number 84-12891
International Standard Book Number 0-8089-1679-3

Printed in the United States of America
85 86 87 88   10 9 8 7 6 5 4 3 2 1

CONTENTS

v

Substance Abuse and Family Therapy is a timely, important, and clinically relevant book worth close study by professionals in the fields of family therapy and substance abuse. It is still common to find family therapists unfamiliar with substance abuse and substance abuse professionals unfamiliar with family therapy. This book should close the knowledge gap.

I have had the advantage of watching Kaufman work on videotape and in person, and actually doing therapy with him. He is a very effective therapist and a good teacher of his clinical methods. The next best thing to working with or observing Kaufman is to read his work. His is an intimate, personal, and even idiosyncratic approach. This is exactly as it should be, for much of our literature on clinical method is so abstract and theoretical that the reader ends up not knowing what the author actually does! On the other hand, Ed Kaufman tells you exactly what he is doing and why he is doing it. This honesty is critical to the improvement of clinical method. We often hide behind benign and banal generalities, or obfuscate our work in the cloak of theoretical rationalizations. This may protect the therapist, but it obviously does nothing to promote critical dialogue.

Reading this book is an experience in dialogue with Kaufman. I trust the reader will enter the book in such a spirit of dialogue.

In the Preface, Kaufman gives a brief history of his own development as a psychoanalyst, family therapist, and clinical expert in substance abuse. This is worth noting because Kaufman is not a "loose eclectic" who is dissatisfied with one field and vaguely tries to latch onto something new that comes along. Quite the contrary, he is a seasoned therapist with many years of clinical experience, and is demanding of himself, his patients, and his readers. He has the ability to grapple with life as it really is in a tough field. From his many years of clinical experience Kaufman has arrived at a perspective he calls *pragmatic psychodynamics*, a theoretical and clinical system that works in the real world of prisons, ghettos, community clinics, alcoholics, and drug addicts.

This is an important issue for a clinical theory, because an abundance of literature is based on limited and selected patient samples drawn from elite academic populations. Since Kaufman and I are both academicians, we obviously do not inveigh against academia. On the other hand, although we have both been trained in formal psychoanalytic and family therapy traditions, we have found those traditions at times lacking in terms of what it takes to make theoretical systems work in the non-academic world.

What Kaufman does in this book is to take psychoanalytic theory and family therapy and merge them into the larger framework of systems analysis. He then demonstrates how to approach the unique clinical problems of substance abuse from this framework. I hasten to assure the reader that just because one is well-trained in psychoanalysis or in family therapy, one is *not* necessarily prepared to treat the unique problems of substance abuse. Let me offer two examples:

- A psychoanalyst friend of mine in another city referred a patient to me for continued treatment. In the first interview, I discovered that the patient was unable to perform his job because of his alcoholism. I asked him what had occurred in his prior five years of analysis in regard to his alcoholism, and he stated that he had never discussed it.
- A group of family therapists were training substance-abuse counselors for family therapy. They told me that they did

not need to know anything about substance abuse in order to train the counselors. When I asked how they would handle the problem of a drunk or "high" family member in a family therapy session, I was told that it was assumed no one in a family treatment program would be abusing drugs or alcohol.

I cite these examples to illustrate that it is not enough to know theory, method, and technique. It is also important to know the clinical problems, which do not come in neat categories anymore. Alcoholics often concomitantly abuse and are dependent on tranquilizers, sedatives, hypnotics, and barbiturates. Methadone maintenance patients may become alcohol-dependent. Many patients are "polymorphous perverse addicts" who engage in drug-abusive and drug-dependent use of many different classes of drugs. All of these patients may connive, confuse, rationalize, deny, obfuscate, and create chaos in general. By this I do not mean to denounce the substance abuser. Rather, I mean to point up the need for the clinician to be an absolute realist. You cannot "pussy-foot" around in this field and expect to be clinically effective. You must deal with the reality of what is going on—action first, analysis second. The clinical treatment of substance abuse is a very rewarding endeavor, but successful treatment only occurs in the context of Kaufman's pragmatic psychodynamics.

Kaufman sets out clinical principles that are based on *both* theory and experience. Do not expect one "party line" from Kaufman. He does an excellent job of blending psychoanalytic, structural, interactional, and behavioral theory and techniques. In fact, he does not just stick with family therapy either. Again, this is as it should be—reflecting what the clinician can and must do in the real world. The effective clinician operates from a reservoir of informed clinical theory that is sensitively applied to different clinical situations.

Why should we concern ourselves with the families of substance abusers? First, substance abuse impacts upon families. Second, families create, promote, and sustain substance abuse. Third, families as a social system may be considered as *substance-abusing* families. Finally, the research literature documents family intervention as the most consistently effective strategy to date for treating substance abuse. That alone merits our close attention to the application of family therapy to substance abuse.

Since this book provides ample discussion and documentation of all these issues, it is superfluous for me to reiterate them any further. My task, a pleasurable one, is to commend Ed Kaufman to you. This is a personal salute to him for writing an excellent and personal book.

E. Mansell Pattison, M.D.
Professor and Chairman
Department of Psychiatry and Health Behavior
Medical College of Georgia,
Augusta, Georgia

Therapy is a complex mixture of theory and application and involves an interplay between the two. Theory determines the use, which in turn modifies the theory. A text on therapy then must reflect the ongoing interaction between theory and practice. The result of this interaction is technique. Our goal in the *Family Therapy* series has been to find people with expertise in both areas and the ability to communicate their knowledge to others.

In our series we have attempted to present a total picture of a subject to a reader whose knowledge is limited. It is a formidable task. Choosing substance abuse as a subject was an obvious one. The problem was deciding whether to produce a contributed piece or the work of one person. The former approach had the advantage of compiling different points of view—and giving the reader much material—but the disadvantage was of not having a critical evaluation. On the other hand, the alternative of selecting one author had the potential disadvantage of presenting a too, narrow viewpoint. The solution, then, was to find someone who could present a broad spectrum so that this disadvantage would be overcome. Many names were suggested and rejected as lacking in one area or another of expertise.

Finally, Dr. Kaufman was selected, and it will be evident why upon reading the text. What will strike the reader most forcefully is an impression of clarity.

Dr. Edward Kaufman has presented us with a superb blending of theory and practice in his volume *Substance Abuse and Family Therapy.* His approach to the field of substance abuse is an eclectic one in the pristine sense of that term, i.e., the best from various sources. In this volume, an amalgam of psychodynamic, systems, and behavioral approaches has been formed into a total picture of a critical problem in American society. Substance abuse is perhaps the most widespread and pressing problem among the social issues of our time.

Dr. Kaufman has utilized every approach as he takes us through a myriad of techniques and gleans from each of them. What is remarkable is his ability to evaluate each one and to see its value and its limitations. There is no one definitive approach but only the ongoing struggle with the problem. The reader of this volume will also gain knowledge of the history and treatment of substance abuse.

The achievement of *Substance Abuse and the Family* is to present a coherent picture of a complex field that touches upon sociology, psychology and anthropology. The reader feels both the breadth and depth of the field due to Kaufman's unified point of view. One illustration of the nuance found in the text is the attention paid to ethnic factors in treatment. Dr. Kaufman is sensitive to the differences that exist among various people and aware of their importance for a successful outcome. One does not find this subtlety in other material on substance abuse.

A final observation is in order. This editor feels he is most knowledgeable in the area of substance abuse; yet the author has produced a text I would gladly call my own. I can think of no greater compliment than to say I am jealous of his ability to combine theory, practice, and technique into a unified picture of a most difficult subject. The reader, upon finishing this text, will no doubt concur with this opinion.

Vincent D. Foley, Ph.D.
Jamaica Estates, New York

My work with the families of substance abusers brings together my many professional directions over the past 25 years. Early in my career I pursued two presumably divergent interests: psychoanalysis and the physiological effects of drug dependence on the sleep–dream cycle. When I attended the Columbia Psychoanalytic Institute, one of the most influential teachers on the faculty was, fortunately, Nathan Ackerman, M.D., who is considered by many the founding father of family therapy. Ackerman taught me how the therapist "repeoples" the family— becomes part of the family system so that the family "takes the therapist home with them" between sessions. More importantly, he encouraged me to be free and spontaneous with families.

At the same time my physiological research brought me to urban ghettos to recruit addicts for subjects, and I became fascinated with addictive disorders. (Withdrawing a heroin addict in the era of potent heroin of the early 1960s was a scary prospect because of severe withdrawal symptoms. Because heroin presently is often 99.5 percent impure, the ease of detoxification has made it less difficult to utilize psychotherapeutic approaches, particularly those involving the family.) My first extensive experience with substance abusers was as a psychiatrist in a federal penitentiary that had a high proportion of heroin addicts and alcoholics. I had little contact with the prisoners' families but began to observe the powerful effects of their social networks on their behavior. Later, as the director of a community psychiatric ward, I rapidly learned how ineffective even the best of traditional psychiatric units is with substance abusers. In my search for effective treatment of heroin addicts, I found Reality House, an intensive day treatment program in New York City, where I consulted for over five years. Although Reality House's treatment philosophy was to deal with the addict in his or her social environment, there was no family involvement, which was typical of such programs in the late 1960s. My first view of the heroin addict's family was through the unidimensional approach of psychoanalytic interviews of heroin addicts at Columbia University in 1970. Subsequently, I directed a psychiatric emergency service, a day hospital, and mental health services in the New York City prison system and gradually began to further my interest in family treatment. In the early 1970s my new friendships and collegial relationships with Peggy Papp and Lynn Hoffman of the Ackerman Institute influenced my view of family intervention. Around the same time, during a national drug abuse meeting, I met Dave Wellisch at a workshop on drug-free approaches to drug abuse (which in those days meant merely that the patient was not on methadone).

In 1971, I decided it was time to devote myself fully to the treatment of substance abuse and I became the medical director of a large multimodality treatment program in New York City, the Lower East Side Service Center (LESC). This program utilized methadone maintenance, drug-free outpatient psychotherapy, a day program with vocational skills training, and a residential therapeutic community. It was at LESC that I began to observe the tremendous involvement of drug abusers with alcohol. At the time I began working with this program, little family therapy was utilized although several therapists had some training and experience in this technique.

Pauline Kaufmann, who was then Director of Family Therapy for Phoenix House, was doing some excellent family work with adolescent substance abusers in the early 1970s. Several Phoenix House graduates who worked with me at LESC insisted that I must meet Pauline because of our ability as mental health professionals to work with and gain the respect of heroin addicts. When I finally did meet her at a workshop she led on family therapy, I realized what had to be done to implement family therapy at LESC. I had to construct a workable system of family treatment for heroin addicts, and I had to begin the actual treatment myself, even if it meant staying until 11 p.m. in order to work with the many families who were eager to receive such treatment. Pauline helped me to learn her system of family treatment. She also helped to convince the disbelievers among the staff at LESC of the need for family therapy as well as assisting in training them.

Pauline and I collaborated on several articles and co-edited a book, *Family Therapy of Drug and Alcohol Abuse* (New York: Gardner Press, 1979.) Pauline, who had been greatly influenced by Salvador Minuchin, recommended that I attend a workshop led by Minuchin and Jay Haley at the Philadelphia Child Guidance Clinic. Their work influenced me so greatly that I rapidly integrated their systems of family therapy into my systems. Also, Duke Stanton was then utilizing structural family therapy at the Philadelphia Child Guidance Clinic, and our professional relationship and friendship have been important in shaping my involvement in family treatment.

For the next four years I conducted a successful multiple family group for heroin addicts, which was an excellent training ground for other family therapists in the program.

In 1977, I moved with my family to California to work at the University of California at Irvine (UCI). In addition I consulted at the Venice Drug Abuse Coalition, as well as the drug detoxification and treatment programs at Metropolitan State Hospital, Orange County Mental Health Drug and Alcohol Programs, and the Care Manor Hospital (recently renamed Care Unit of Orange).

It became very important to me to learn as much as I possibly could about the family therapy of substance abuse so that I could give the knowledge back to the individuals I was teaching. Thus my prime teachers became my patients and students. In addition, I was fortunate in teaming with Judith Anderson and Linda Borders, who became co-teachers, co-therapists, and co-learners as we explored and taught the many new developments in family therapy that have evolved over the past few years. Dr. Anderson and I founded and co-direct the family therapy section of UCI's Department of Psychiatry. Linda Borders and I developed the family therapy program at the Huntington Beach Child Guidance Clinic.

My involvement with Care Manor increased during my early years in California, which led to my seeing more and more families that had alcoholism as a primary problem and consequently to my more recent interest in alcoholism.

Most recently, I have become associated with the excellent university-based drug and alcohol program at Capistrano by the Sea Hospital in Dana Point. The university environment that has surrounded me these past seven years has greatly stimulated my interest in the quantitative assessment of the families of substance abusers and their treatment. The emphasis on scientific vigor has also helped me to clarify my thinking as an observer of these families as well as develop a clearer system of family-based intervention.

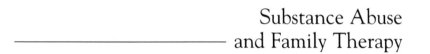

Substance Abuse
and Family Therapy

Part I

INTRODUCTION

Chapter 1

Definition of the Problem, Personality, and Psychopathology

There can be little doubt that we live in a society in which drugs and alcohol are viewed as our major means to relieve pain, fear, and boredom. The use, misuse, and abuse of alcohol and other drugs is presently rampant and is continuing to increase. Alcoholism ranks as the third most prevalent public health problem in our society. The number of alcoholics and alcohol abusers in this country has been repeatedly estimated at nine to ten million. One third of Americans have alcohol problems in their families. Alcohol-related highway crashes kill over 25,000 persons a year, including 10,000 youths between age 16 and 24 (National Institute of Alcohol and Alcohol Abuse, 1982) and seriously injure 300,000 others yearly. Adding to these numbers are alcohol-related diseases. Alcoholism is the third most common health problem and the fifth leading cause of death in the United States (Cohen, 1978). In contrast to most illicit drug use, alcohol exerts a tremendous effect on the working population. The economic loss to the nation from alcohol problems is at least $15 billion yearly. Six percent of twelfth-graders drink daily (National Institute of Alcohol and Alcohol Abuse). One of every 6 teenagers and one of every 11 Americans suffers from a severe problem with substance abuse (Cummings, 1979). Over 90 million prescriptions are filled yearly for minor tranquilizers.

Prescription and black market barbiturates, stimulants, and newer synthetic sleeping medications are widely abused. The problems caused by use of these "pills" are in many ways greater than those caused by the 500,000 heroin addicts in our society, despite the publicity given the latter. The damage done by pills, booze, and cocaine is extremely expensive when viewed from the point of difficulties caused for the substance-abusing individual and his/or her immediate family. Substance abuse continues despite a recent growing and important thrust to educate the public to the dangers of substance abuse and the alternatives that are available, such as exercise and counseling.

Some individuals use, misuse, and abuse alcohol and drugs without becoming dependent or being defined as alcoholics or addicts. However, these patterns contribute to health impairment, family dysfunction, vehicular and pedestrian accidents, criminal behavior, destructive social behavior, and other adverse consequences. Alcohol and drug problems are therefore not limited to the individuals themselves.

Alcohol and pills are part of our "over-medicated society," in which the use of psychoactive substances of many kinds are viewed as personally desirable and socially acceptable. The current widespread use of alcohol is supported by legal, personal, professional, social, and cultural sanctions. There is similar support for the use of prescription mind-altering drugs. There are few social rules or guidelines about the safe and proper use of alcohol or sedatives or about the avoidance, deterrence, and adverse consequences of these substances. Substance abuse is no respecter of age, sex, ethnicity, geography, or legality (Pattison & Kaufman, 1982).

Substance abuse is defined as the use of a psychoactive drug, alcohol, or a combination of the two to the extent that it seriously interferes with an individual's physical health, social relationships, or vocational functioning. The Diagnostic and Statistical Manual (DSM III, 1980) classifies a syndrome of substance use disorders, dividing the problem into substance abuse and dependence. DSM III criteria for abuse are a pattern of pathological use, impairment in social or occupational functioning due to substance use, and a minimal duration of disturbance of at least one month. Substance dependence is diagnosed if there is either tolerance or withdrawal and for a diagnosis of alcohol or marijuana dependence, a pattern of pathological use and/or social or occupational impairment. However, for the purposes of this book, the term *substance abuse* is used instead of the less familiar *substance use disorders*. Substance abuse, as used in this book, may include dependence as well as abuse, but often the two are described separately. In addition, the phrases *heroin addicts* and *drug addicts* generally will be used instead of more techically correct "drug-dependent individuals" because the former is so commonly used.

Alcohol and drug disease states may be diagnosed in two major ways: binary and multivariate. (Pattison & Kaufman, 1982) The binary approach is based on the idea that one clearly is or is not an alcoholic or drug addict. The problem with this approach is that it assumes that these terms apply to a distinct class of persons who have a specific disease rather than to a diverse set of behavioral problems. The research observations of the past 20 years clearly demonstrate that the all-or-nothing concept of alcoholism and drug abuse is incorrect.

Most scientific authorities in the field of alcoholism and drug abuse now concur that alcoholism and drug abuse are most accurately construed as a multivariate syndrome. That is, there are multiple patterns of dysfunctional use that occur in various types of personalities, with multiple combinations of adverse consequences, with multiple prognoses, that may require different types of treatment interventions (Pattison & Kaufman, 1982).

ABUSE OF DRUGS AND ALCOHOL IN COMBINATION

This book deals with the combined problems of drugs and alcohol abuse because so many people in our society abuse both drugs and alcohol. In addition, the families of drug abusers and alcoholics are similar in many ways and at times are the same families viewed from different generations. As will be demonstrated in Chapters 2, 3, and 4, many families with alcoholic parents have children who present as drug abusers and/or alcoholics.

People have used combinations of drugs and alcohol for centuries. However, starting in about 1970, a growing trend to alternate or simultaneously abuse alcohol and a multitude of other drugs was observed (Kaufman, 1977). The literature on the families of alcoholics and the families of drug abusers and addicts emerged separately and appeared to describe very different types of family systems. When these families were examined closely, we learned that very frequently we were dealing with the same family but focusing on different generations, like the parable of three blind men touching different parts of the elephant. Thus the literature on the alcoholic family tended to focus on a 45-year-old male alcoholic, his spouse and his adolescent (frequently drug-abusing) progeny. The literature on the drug abuser tended to focus on a young man in his late teens or early twenties and his parents, one or both of whom were alcoholic in at least half of the reported cases. The focus of this book is on the three- or four-generational system of the families of substance abusers, regardless of the age and substance or substances of choice of the identified patient. Thus, we will look at the grandparents, parents, siblings, and progeny of the substance abuser as well as at the extended kinship system. We will also look carefully at the different effects of female versus male substance abuse on the family system as well as the specific needs of females in treatment.

The combined use of alcohol and drugs can be classified into four categories (Kaufman, 1977): (1) the abuse of drugs by alcoholics and problem drinkers, (2) the abuse of alcohol by drug abusers and dependents, (3) "polydrug abuse," which includes alcohol, and (4) the use of alcohol as a steppingstone to other drugs.

THE ABUSE OF DRUGS BY ALCOHOLICS AND PROBLEM DRINKERS

In an excellent review of the literature from 1925 to 1972, Freed (1973) noted that drug abuse by alcoholics ranged from 5 percent to 52 percent and concluded that at least 20 percent of alcoholics used at least one other dependence-prone drug. As evidence of the increasing use of drugs by alcoholics, Rosenberger (1969) noted that young alcoholics tend to abuse multiple drugs (52 percent) much more frequently than do older alcoholics (16 percent). The media of the late 1970s described that the youth of America were giving up drugs and switching back to alcohol. Schnoll's (1979) synthesis of the literature emphasized that this is not the case, rather, there is an ever-increasing use of alcohol and other drugs. Another consistent trend is that illicit drug abuse is much higher in heavy alcohol users than in light drinkers (Wechsler & Thum, 1973). There is also a considerably higher use of drugs by incarcerated than non-imprisoned criminal alcoholics (Carrol, Malloy, & Kendrick, 1980). In a study of alcoholism treatment programs funded by the National Institute of Alcohol and Alcohol Abuse (NIAAA) in 1975 (Tuckfield, McLeroy, & Waterhose, 1975) it was noted that 30 to 60 percent of all clients were using drugs in addition to alcohol at the time of admission, and about half of these were abusing these drugs. Most of these drugs were obtained by prescription from private physicians. This study also confirmed that the phenomenon was more common in those under age 30.

Dependence on drugs by alcoholics is obviously less frequent than drug use itself. In several studies cited by Carroll et al. (1980) drug dependence in alcoholics ranged from 10 to 50 percent. Female alcoholics as a discrete category have not been studied with respect to drug abuse until quite recently. Corrigan (1980) noted that 82 percent of women alcoholics have used other drugs in addition to alcohol. About half used other drugs while drinking. Of these, 42 percent used tranquilizers or sedatives, 24 percent sleeping pills, and 15 percent stimulants. As with men, very heavy drinkers and those under age 30 run a considerably higher risk of combining other drugs with alcohol. However, women alcoholics generally abuse far more prescription drugs than do their male counterparts.

Alcoholics often substitute narcotics for alcohol when the former are readily available. Many alcoholics readily become dependent on codeine when prescribed by physicians in the same way that they do on sedatives and tranquilizers. In a study of 451 US Army enlisted men after their return from Vietnam, Goodwin, Davis, and Robins (1975) noted that prior to enlistment, nearly half had been regular drinkers, 25 percent had drinking problems, and 4 percent were alcoholics. Problem drinking declined in Vietnam (75 percent decreased their drinking) as opiate use rose (50 percent tried opiates and 20 percent were opiate dependent). After Vietnam, opiate use and dependence decreased (less than 2 percent were opiate dependent) and problem drinking again became ascendant (33 percent had drinking problems and 8 percent were alcoholic).

Wesson, Carlin, Adams, and Beschner (1978) in their national study noted that approximately 11 percent of those individuals who presented for treatment at agencies specializing in alcoholism also had concomitant and significant amounts of non-opiate drug abuse. At the Care Unit Hospital of Orange, a shift to combined abuse of drugs and alcohol has been noted over the past five years. The percentage of patients with combined problems in the first six months of 1977 was 6.4 percent. In 1980 the percentage rose to 17.3 percent, and in 1982 to 32.8 percent. Busto (1982) found that one third of alcoholic patients (48 percent of females, 29 percent of males) in an outpatient clinic had benzodiazepines in their urine and at least half of these were abusers. This confirms my own experience, which is that prescribing dependence-prone drugs of any kind to alcoholics in outpatient settings carries a high risk of abuse and dependency.

It should also be noted that personal reports by alcoholics tend to under-report drug use. However, when the urine of alcoholics is routinely monitored for drugs, the incidence of drug use is much higher: 38 percent by urinalysis as compared to 9 percent by self-report (Chelton & Whisnant, 1966).

The Abuse of Alcohol by Drug Abusers and Dependents

Heroin Addicts

Over the past decade there has been an increase in the use of alcohol by heroin addicts. The phenomenon itself is by no means a new one, and the quantitative increase in alcohol use may simply be a direct result of the decreasing purity of available heroin. In addition, the more a heroin addict abuses multiple drugs, the more likely he or she is to abuse alcohol as well (Richman, 1976).

Barr and Cohen (1980) found the prevalence of heavy drinkers among drug addicts to be 50.3 percent. Baden (1974) noted that narcotism plus alcoholism was the cause of death in 10 percent of narcotic-related deaths in the 1950s and had risen to 20 percent in 1972. In Orange County, California in 1976, heroin and alcohol accounted for 40 percent of narcotic deaths, and heroin plus drugs for another 12 percent.

Methadone Maintenance Patients

Drinking by heroin addicts during participation in methadone maintenance treatment has been studied in depth. Gearing (1973) noted that 10 percent of such patients abuse alcohol. Kreek (1973) estimated that 12 percent of methadone maintenance patients (MMPs) consume more than 12 ounces of alcohol daily and that 13 percent consume 4–12 ounces daily. Gelb, Richman, and Deyser (1979) in a study of 101 MMPs found that 12 percent consumed 3 or more ounces of alcohol per day. Stimmel, Cohen, and Hanbury (1978) noted that the prevalence of alcohol abuse in methadone maintenance patients varied from 10 to 40 percent, with some investigators noting that alcohol abuse increases by 100 percent after initiating a maintenance program. Barr and Cohen (1980) found that 13.7 percent of 586 MMPs had high levels of alcohol consumption and problems stemming from alcohol. However, another 16.6 percent had high alcohol consumption with few or no problems.

Alcohol abuse by MMPs is a major factor in the high incidence of liver damage in these patients. Gelb, Richman, and Anand (1978) determined that in 68 percent of alcohol-abusing MMPs, regular alcohol abuse preceded narcotic use. Alcohol abuse began after start of treatment in 29 percent of alcohol-abusing MMPs.

Thus although alcohol abuse may precede or follow the start of a maintenance program, there is no doubt that alcoholism is a serious problem among methadone patients. This is particularly true for those who stay in treatment for several years and do not sustain meaningful intrapsychic as well as social, familial, and vocational changes.

Polydrug Abusers

The term "polydrug" was introduced in the 1970s to describe the phenomenon of abuse and dependence on a combination of drugs and alcohol. As defined by the National Institute of Drug Abuse, the term came to mean drug abuse wherein the primary drug problem was not heroin, methadone, or alcohol. However, when Wesson et al. (1978) studied polydrug abuse treatment programs in America, they found that the modal polydrug abuse pattern was that of an individual who uses non-opiates, alcohol, and narcotic drugs in various combinations. This combined use of different drugs and alcohol, in which there is no clear substance of choice, is what we presently term "polydrug abuse." As treatment programs labelled specifically for polydrug abuse treatment have disappeared, these individuals now present themselves to programs that primarily treat either drug abusers or alcoholics.

The National Youth Polydrug Study (Santo, Farley, & Friedman, 1980) noted that alcohol was second only to marijuana as the substance most regularly used by youths in treatment for polydrug abuse (79.8 percent versus 85.9 percent). However, weekly users of both marijuana and alcohol reported having used an average of slightly more than three other substances on a regular weekly basis.

Polydrug abuse is also seen in psychiatric patients. Crowley, Chesluk, Dilts and Hart (1974) found that over one third of adults in a psychiatric hospital had drug and/or alcohol problems. They found that recent alcohol use was associated with the use of cocaine, sedative-hypnotics, and antianxiety drugs. Conversely, they also found that heavy users of antianxiety drugs used alcohol excessively.

Alcohol as a Steppingstone to Other Drugs

The steppingstone hypothesis was originally presented as a primary danger of marijuana—that it led to use of "hard" drugs, particularly heroin. However, alcohol has been found to be a more common precursor and therefore a steppingstone to heroin dependence. Schut, File, and Wohlmuth (1973) showed that 97 of 100 heroin addicts reported using alcohol prior to drugs. Rosen, Ottenberg, and Barr (1975) similarly reported that alcohol was the first substance abused by 89 percent of 183 subjects. Greene (1980), in a survey of 1544 subjects, found that 94 percent of regular users of heroin were at some point in time regular users of alcohol. He found that 72 percent of regular users of heroin first used alcohol on a regular basis. He also noted that 65 percent of marijuana abusers also used alcohol first on a regular basis.

Longitudinal surveys indicate four stages in the sequence of involvement with drugs. The progression is from beer to wine or both to cigarettes or hard liquor, then to marijuana and then to illicit drugs (Kandel, 1975). I propose that neither alcohol nor marijuana is truly a steppingstone in seducing a nonpredisposed individual down the path to "hard" drugs. Rather, they are both very commonly used in our society and are used and abused sequentially and more frequently by those who are predisposed to eventually go on to "harder drugs." It is understandable that such behaviorally and biologically vulnerable individuals would first try the more available less dangerous drugs before they try the less available and more risky drugs (Schuckit, 1973).

Thus we see the commonality of usage of drugs by alcoholics and alcohol by drug abusers which demonstrate how studies of an alcoholic's family system at one point in time may really be evaluating a family which at some other point in time was the family of a drug abuser or vice versa. The ubiquitous nature of inextricably woven drug and alcohol abuse compels us to look at both problems together as well as to attempt to tease them apart.

PROFILE OF MALE SUBSTANCE ABUSERS

Psychopathology

Substance abuse is a final common pathway for many different types of individuals with varied personalities and psychiatric diagnoses. (This section deals mainly with males, as

Chapter 4 will be devoted to female substance abusers.) The prevalence of overt psychopathology in alcoholics and drug abusers is extremely variable, depending on diagnostic criteria and sample variability. We must also differentiate Axis I disorders like psychosis and neurosis from Axis II personality disorders like borderline and antisocial. The diagnoses of schizophrenia in alcoholics ranges from 1 to 49 percent (Freed, 1973). About 25 percent of alcoholics studied in hospital emergency rooms were found to have an antisocial personality (Khantzian, 1982). Evidence of sociopathy was found prior to clinical alcoholism in 37 percent of male and 22 percent of female alcoholics (Woodruff, Guze, Clayton, & Carr, 1973). The incidence of depression in alcoholism is even more variably estimated than of schizophrenia, ranging from 3 to 98 percent (Khantzian, 1982). Weisman, Meyers, and Harding (1980) reported that 71 percent of 34 alcoholics had at some time received another psychiatric diagnosis, mainly depression. My own diagnostic studies of drug addicts showed that 48 percent of an upper-socioeconomic-group sample were borderline or overtly psychotic by DSM II criteria. Similarly disturbed were 25 percent of a mixed social group but only 3 percent of a lower-class group (Kaufman, 1976). When major psychiatric illness such as schizophrenia or severe depression is found in substance abusers, the treatment of psychiatric illness must have a high priority. (Substance abusers tend to regress to more severe levels of psychopathology after long-term abuse.)

Several prospective studies of alcoholics have been performed. Kammeier, Hoffman, and Loper (1973) studied the Minnesota Multiphasic Personality Inventories (MMPIs) of a group of 38 male alcoholics 13 years prior to treatment. Although psychological maladjustment was not found, this group of pre-alcoholics had significantly higher sociopathic and manic scores, and were more impulsive and less conforming than their peers. Vaillant (1980) followed up 184 college students at age 50. He found that early relationships with parents, childhood psychological problems (bleak childhoods), and psychological well-being and anxiety levels in college did not differentiate social drinkers from those who became alcohol abusers. However, men with childhood psychological problems were twice as likely to use mood-altering drugs regularly.

Personality

There are personality characteristics which are more or less specific to alcoholics, others to drug abusers, and some which are seen in both types of substance abusers. However, these will vary with other factors such as age, gender, social class, ethnicity, and stage of abuse or dependence. Most of the studies describing these personality characteristics have been performed on males after years of substance abuse and dependence. It is important for the family therapist to be aware of the personality types seen in substance abusers, as these characteristics greatly influence behavior in the family and in family therapy.

Similarities Between Drug Abusers and Alcoholics

It is easier to describe the common aspects of drug abusers and alcoholics than it is to tease out those that are unique. Both groups excessively rely on similar defense mechanisms including regression, denial, introjection, projection, and rationalization. Lying is common in both groups. At times reality and memory are so blurred that lying is often unintentional.

Both drugs and alcohol are used to diminish anxieties about self-assertion in work and social contacts. Sedative drugs and alcohol are used to obliterate anger and hostility, which are, however, released during intoxication. Drug abusers and alcoholics are impulsive, with a low frustration tolerance and an inability to endure anxiety or tension. There frequently is a schizoid adjustment with social fears and low self-esteem (Fox, 1975), which is covered over during intoxication. Drug and alcohol abusers both have repressed or conscious feelings of omnipotence and gradiosity, little ability to persevere and follow through, and extreme narcissism. Marked unaccountable mood swings are present (and not necessarily indicative of mood cycle disease). There is a constant inner battle between passivity and aggressiveness and sexual impulses, and strong dependent needs are inevitably frustrated, leading to depression, despair or hostility, rage, and fantasies of revenge (Fox, 1975).

A survey of over 2000 alcoholics compared with a non-alcoholic group from the general population revealed that alcoholics tend to be only children and last borns from large sub-ships. (Conley, 1980). This finding is similar to Kaufman and Kaufmann's (1979) study of heroin addicts, which showed a majority of youngest and only children. This phenomenon may be explained by the permissiveness with which youngest and only children are raised (Conley, 1980) or by the family's need to have a baby to take care of or deflect marital issues when there are no other children present.

Khantzian (1982) described the ego deficit in substance abusers as an inability to handle emotions, coupled with over- or under-control. He also noted a tendency in these individuals to overestimate or underestimate their worth and an inability to maintain an inner sense of cohesiveness, self-comfort, or well-being. Khantzian (1982) attributed the severe dependence in substance abusers to ego deficits and vulnerability rather than to oral cravings. In the minority of alcoholics and drug abusers who are seriously mentally disturbed, these substances provide a sense of internal homeostasis which substitutes for the basic lack of a sense of integration of self (Kaufman, 1976).

When both types of abusers give up their substances, there is a prolonged period of physiological withdrawal (6–12 months) as well as a potentially longer psychological mourning period for the lost substances. They expect all kinds of rewards for giving up their precious substance and become furious when rewards are not received, which leads in part to the family problems that follow sobriety and drug-free states.

Personality Characteristics of Alcoholics

Alcoholics tend to show more depression and guilt, higher levels of anxiety, more authority conflicts, more passivity, and more neurotic traits than non-alcoholics or heroin addicts. They are also more emotionally labile and less independent (Craig, 1982). The denial that alcoholics show is extremely rigid and does not readily shift with confrontation, perhaps because of underlying ego fragility. There is also a strong archaic, punitive superego, causing a tendency toward harsh condemnation, a sense of unworthiness and guilt, and masochistic, self-punitive behavior, (Fox, 1975). The same study also described psychological impotence, ego fragility, sexual immaturity and excessive homosexual conflicts (Fox, 1975). However, later research efforts have tended to disprove these last two characteristics. Many theorists have emphasized that alcoholics drink to satisfy hidden dependency needs that they can not express as adults. Another major dynamic often cited is that they drink to experience a false sense of power over others (Sandmaier, 1980).

Studies of alcoholics scored by the Minnesota Multiphasic Personality Inventory (MMPI) have consistently shown two clear subgroups, one characterized by anxiety and depression, the other by antisocial characteristics (Khantzian, 1982). The MacAndrew Alcoholism Scale has identified these MMPI characteristics of alcoholics that do not change with drinking cycles (MacAndrew, 1965).

Alcoholics tend to become overly dependent on a therapist in individual psychotherapy. This problem is ameliorated in family therapy because the dependency conflicts are worked on within the family.

Personality Characteristics of Drug Abusers

Although a minority of drug abusers and addicts have strong superegos (and these individuals have a good prognosis), the majority have absent or severely limited superegos and strong antisocial proclivities. Antisocial drug abusers tend to be more overtly aggressive when not intoxicated than do alcoholics. Although many drug abusers use drugs to overcome or mask sexual conflicts, they tend to have fewer underlying conflicts about sexuality than alcoholics. The illegality of most drug use forces them into greater antisocial acts, and resultant extended incarceration leads to reinforcement of antisocial behavior (Kaufman, 1974). Although they form dependent relationships, they shift their dependency readily from one person to another, as from mother to wife to lover or from therapist to therapist.

A heroin scale was developed for the MMPI, originally to identify addicts in a prison population. This scale deals with depressed emotional tones, ambivalent religious attitudes, resentment of authority, confused psychological development, denial, cunningness, and grandiosity (Craig, 1982). Heroin addicts have higher mean scores on this scale than alcoholics, but polydrug abusers score higher than both (Lachar, Berman, Grisell and Schoof 1979). Heroin addicts are more independent and aggressive and have greater ego strength than alcoholics (Craig, 1982).

Khantzian (1980) noted the lifelong preoccupation of heroin addicts with aggression, and felt that heroin is used specifically as an antiaggression drug. Wurmser (1980) stated that alcohol or "drug use is pre-eminently a pharmacologically reinforced denial" in that it attempts to diminish the feeling impact of painful inner and outer reality. Wurmser noted that addicts defend against their phobic core by seeking an external object (heroin) as a protector and consistently use the defense of turning passive into active. Years before beginning my family studies of drug abuse, I conducted a study consisting of psychodynamic interviews of college students who were heroin addicts. In this group I noted the following psychological aspects (Kaufman, 1974):

> Frequent masturbatory fantasies about mother as well as overt sexual attraction to her were common in male addicts. Several siblings were also opiate dependents and in most of these cases there was a symbiotic tie between the addict siblings. When first used, heroin frequently facilitated sexual performance through physiological retardation of ejaculation or by psychological relaxation. In later phases there was little concern with sex. Heroin was also frequently used to facilitate assertion or communication. However, in later phases there was little concern with either assertion or communication. Several patients had masochistic fantasies as their major repetitive fantasy and two had histories of serious self-multilation. One student felt that his ability to use the needle represented his only area of personal competence. Several students frequently dealt with fears of death by counter-phobicly coming close to death through overdoses. The use of heroin represented the ultimate parental defiance as well as peer status through use of the 'king of drugs.' Three students were political activists. One student with a severe clinical depression used heroin as an antidepressant.

Heroin was frequently used to neutralize murderous aggressive fantasies. For several, the act of injecting heroin represented a type of sexual gratification. Heroin frequently provided a primitive homeostasis which helped reconstitute a feeling of total bodily disintegration. Most students had abused many drugs and several alternated heroin and amphetamines, using the latter to permit functioning during final examinations. Many individuals in this study were multidrug dependents rather than specifically dependent on heroin.

Behavior such as low frustration tolerance, viewing other individuals only as providers of supplies, manipulativeness, extractiveness, self-destructiveness, and impaired reality testing historically had been taken as evidence of the addict's oral character structure. These characterological traits occur in all opiate addicts regardless of social class. However, most of these traits are secondary to the addiction rather than a cause of it particularly in ghetto addicts. They invariably develop once an individual becomes addicted to a drug. At this point, he/she can have no value in relationships with others but to find the funds and drugs which are necessary to maintain his/her habit.

Specific Personality and Choice of Abusing Substance

My general premise is that no specific personality type can be attributed to abusers of specific drugs. This is in agreement with Rado (1956), who stated that all types of drug craving were varieties of a single disease called "pharmacothymia." However, several recent findings offer evidence in contradiction to this premise. Milkman and Frosch (1973) found a difference in heroin addicts and amphetamine abusers who had experienced both drugs and expressed a specific preference for one of the two. They demonstrated that individuals for whom heroin was the drug of choice suffer from depression and despair and relieve anxiety by withdrawal and repression of conflict through satiation by the drug. In contrast, those who chose amphetamines have a need to feel active and potent in an environment they perceive as hostile and threatening. The dynamic distinctions are more characteristic of distinctions between stimulants and sedatives in general than between specific drugs. These distinctions do not consider that many individuals who have abused both heroin and amphetamine do not have a clear drug of choice. In a later elaboration of their work, Milkman and Frosch (1980) noted that the heroin addict is given to sporadic rages and tantrums, whereas in the amphetamine user impulse expression is less direct, pervasive, and frequent, and there is preoccupation with violent fantasy when intoxicated. Ego strength is greater in amphetamine abusers and they are able to channel anger more adaptively. Heroin addicts need heroin to dampen drive energies and reduce external stimuli. However, Milkman and Frosch also noted many similarities between the two classes of users, including low self-esteem and feelings of helplessness and anxiety. These symptoms were relieved by taking drugs. These researchers also described a need for immediate rewards without regard to long-term detrimental consequences.

The work of Spotts and Shontz (1980) has developed a differential life theme in abusers of different drugs. Though their work may be criticized as to its generalizability because of the small, regionalized case sample they used, they studied each case in great depth and over an 18-month period. Their work is presented because it is extremely interesting and presents many worthy hypotheses about personality and family differences which deserve further investigation. The chronic amphetamine users they studied reported that they grew up in families with relatively strong but highly manipulative mothers and passive or ineffectual fathers. These mothers were described as devious, ensnaring, deceitful, castrating women who kept their men firmly under control. Thus as adults, these amphetamine users feared women and perceived them as creatures to be conquered, overcome, used, and exploited. They were driven, achievement-oriented men who were strongly reactive against threats of weakness or impotence (Spotts & Shontz, 1980).

In contrast, the narcotic abusers Spotts and Shontz studied described psychologically disabled families in which one parent (usually the father) was absent or an overpowering tyrant while the other parent was too weak to protect the subject child from the attacks of the strong parent. As adults, the opiate users were seriously disabled, with weak, poorly differentiated egos, but no distinctive set of symptoms. They were vulnerable, quiet, lonely, and unambitious and sought "a tranquil, serene existence through ego constriction." Their Q-sort data revealed a pervasive, underlying depression.

In the same study, cocaine users described their mothers as warm and their fathers as strong and encouraging and their early family lives as highly positive overall. As adults, they had stronger, more resilient egos than men in the other drug use groups. They were ambitious, intensely competitive men who worked hard to become successful, took risks, and lived by their wits. Their need to be completely self-sufficient was compensation for their intensely denied dependency needs.

The barbiturate users, whom Spotts & Shontz felt are similar to alcoholics, grew up lacking meaningful relationships with either parent. Most described families with "uninteresting, neglecting fathers and timorous, dependent and ineffectual mothers". These subjects repeatedly performed acts which seemingly tempted fate to destroy them. "Each succeeding setback and reversal adds to the gradual disintegration of the self. By reducing ego inhibitions these drugs provide the false courage which permits them to release pent-up destructive forces." These drugs (and alcohol) provide a "ticket for oblivion", which permits denial of failure and releases inhibitions. These, in turn facilitate tension release through fights and accidents with blackouts for the episodes so there is little guilt. Spotts and Shontz felt that the barbiturate users they studied met the criteria for borderline personalities.

Carrol and Zuckerman (1977) studied psychopathology in "downers," "speeders," and "trippers" using the MMPI and the sensation seeking scale. They found that stimulant use was associated with high scores on the hypochondriasis, hysteria, paranoia, schizophrenia, and hypomania scales. Hallucinogen use correlated with the F (confusion, carelessness, or self-depreciation), hypochrondriasis, depression, hysteria, paranoia, psychoasthenia, schizophrenia, and social introversion scales. Experience-seeking was related to stimulant and hallucinogen use and negatively related to depressant use.

Most of the authors who support the hypothesis of specific personality types in users who consistently prefer particular drugs look to a preference based on the specific psychopharmacologic effects interacting with the unique personality and physiologic reactions of the individual (Khantzian, 1980). Khantzian (1980) stated that narcotics "counteract regressed disorganized and dysphoric ego states related to overwhelming feelings of rage, anger and related depression."

In contrast, the amphetamines, hypnotics, and alcohol mobilize the expression of anger and sexual feelings. Wurmser (1980) stated that a drug is chosen to neutralize an affect. For instance, narcotics and hypnotics neutralize rage, shame, and jealousy as well as the anxiety related to these feelings; stimulants neutralize depression and weakness; psychedelics counteract boredom; and alcohol works against guilt, loneliness, and related anxiety. Hendin (1980) found that college men used marijuana specifically "to help ease or withdraw from competitive pressure."

There are a number of common myths about the psychological and physiological effects of specific drugs. For example, drugs such as methaqualone (Quaalude), cocaine, and amphetamines are thought to augment and or improve sexual performance. Actually they may relax a tense individual or activate a passive one so that he or she is able to overcome sexual inhibitions. Heroin has a reputation for dampening sexual drives; however, many heroin abusers find that heroin initially aids sexual performance through psychic relaxation or physiologic retardation of ejaculation. Many heroin users take their first dose with friends before a dance or party to deal with anxieties about social contacts. Many abusers of opiates and sedatives use these drugs to alleviate anxiety about self-assertion, particularly vocational performance. Sedatives and narcotics are frequently used to obliterate anger and avoid hostile confrontation. Unfortunately, when individuals become intoxicated on sedatives or alcohol, rage is frequently released in uncontrolled and destructive ways.

Recent findings of specific receptors in the brain for opiates, amphetamines, methylphenidate (Ritalin), benzodiazepines, and possibly a host of other psychoactive drugs may lead to a strong, neurochemical basis for drug preference related to receptor sensitivity or deficits in endogenous psychoactive substances which is unrelated to personality or psychopathology. Further research in this biological aspect of drug abuse may reveal a great deal about specific organic etiologies of abuse of various drugs and substantially contribute to their treatment in the next decade.

Studies that emphasize different intrapsychic bases for the use of different drugs overlook many important social factors, particularly when sampling is restricted to a social class or limited ethnicity. Social determinants lead to drug abuse when there is a paucity of alternatives to a meaningful life, as in urban ghettoes. In addition, cycles of limited and excessive availability of specific drugs have encouraged the use of other drugs or drug/alcohol combinations. Rather than relating specific drug choice to type of psychopathology, I feel that the more alien a pattern of drug abuse to an individual's social background, the more likely the individual is to be suffering from severe psychopathology (Kaufman, 1976).

———————————————————————— REFERENCES

Baden, M.M., & Haberman, P.W. Drinking, drugs and death. *International Journal of Addiction*, 1974, *9*(6), 761–775.

Barr, H.L., & Cohen, A. The problem drinking drug addict. In S. Gardner (Ed.), *National drug/alcohol collaborative project: Issues in multiple substance abuse*. Department of Health, Education and Welfare, 1980, 78–115.

Busto, U. Benzodiazepines said to be commonly used and abused by alcoholics. *Clinical Psychiatry News*, 1982, *10*(6), 39.

Carrol, E.N., & Zuckerman, M. Psychopathology and sensation seeking in "downers," "speeders," and "trippers": A study of the relationship between personality and drug choice. *International Journal of Addiction*, 1977, *12*(4), 591–601.

Carrol, J.F.X., Malloy, T.E., & Kendrick, F.M. Multiple substance abuse: A review of the literature. In S. Gardner (Ed.), *National drug/alcohol collaborative project: Issues in multiple substance abuse*. Department of Health, Education and Welfare, 1980, 9–24.

Chelton, G.L., & Whisnant, C.L. The combination of alcohol and drug intoxication. *Southern Medical Journal*, 1966, *59*, 393.

Cohen, S. Trends in substance abuse. *Drug Abuse and Alcoholism Newsletter*, 1978, *7*(7), 1–4.

Conley, J.J. Family configuration as an etiological factor in alcoholism. *Journal of Abnormal Psychology*. 1980, *89*(5), 670–673.

Corrigan, E.M. *Alcoholic women in treatment*. New York: Oxford Press, 1980.

Craig, R.J. Personality characteristics of heroin addicts: Review of empirical research, 1976–1979. *International Journal of Addiction*, 1982, *17*(2), 227–248.

Crowley, T.J., Chesluk, D., Dilts, S. & Hart, R. Drug and alcohol abuse among psychiatric admissions. *Archives of General Psychiatry*, 1974, *30*, 13–20.

Cummings, N.A. Turning bread into stones: Our modern antimiracle. *American Psychologist*, 1979, *34*, 1119–1129.

Diagnostic and statistical manual of mental disorders (third edition). Wash, D.C., American Psychiatric Association, 1980.

Fox, R. Group psychotherapy with alcoholics. (In M. Rosenbaum & M.M. Berger (Eds.), *Group psychotherapy and group function.* New York: Basic Books, 1975, 521–528.

Freed, E.X. Drug abuse by alcoholics: A review. *International Journal of Addiction,* 1973, *8,* 451–473.

Gearing, F.R. Myth versus fact in long term methadone maintenance treatment: The community's viewpoint. Proceedings of 5th National Conference on Methadone treatment, New York, Napan, 1973, 452–455.

Gelb, A.M., Richman, B.L., & Anand, O.P. Quantitative and temporal relationships of alcohol use in narcotic addicts and methadone maintenance patients undergoing alcohol detoxification. *American Journal of Drug and Alcohol Abuse,* 1978, *5*(2), 191–198.

Gelb, A.M., Richman, B.L., & Deyser, N.P. Alcohol use in methadone maintenance clinics. *American Journal of Drug and Alcohol Abuse,* 1979, *6*(3), 367–373.

Goodwin, D.W.. Davis, D.H., & Robins, L.N. Drinking amid abundant illicit drugs. *Archives of General Psychiatry* 1975, *32,* 230–233.

Greene, B.T. Sequential use of drugs and alcohol: A reexamination of the steppingstone hypothesis. *American Journal of Drug and Alcohol Abuse,* 1980, *7*(1), 83–99.

Hendin, H. Psychosocial theory of drug abuse: A psychodynamic approach. In D.J. Letteiri, M. Sayers, & H.W. Pearson (Eds.), *Theories on drug abuse: Selected contemporary perspectives.* Rockville, Md.: National Institute on Drug Abuse Research Monograph 30, March 1980, 195–200.

Kammeier, M.C., Hoffman, H., & Loper, R.G. Personality characteristics of alcoholics as college freshman and at time of treatment. *Quarterly Journal of Studies of Alcoholism,* 1973, *34,* 390–399.

Kandel, D. Stages in adolescent involvement in drug use. *Science,* 1975, *190,* 912–914.

Kaufman, E. The psychodynamics of opiate dependence: A new look. *American Journal of Drug and Alcohol Abuse,* 1974, *1,* 349–370.

Kaufman, E. The abuse of multiple drugs. II. Psychological hypotheses, treatment considerations. *American Journal of Drug and Alcohol Abuse,* 1976, *3*(2), 293–301.

Kaufman, E. Polydrug abuse or multidrug misuse: It's here to stay. *British Journal of Addiction,* 1977, *72,* 339–347.

Kaufman, E., & Kaufmann, P. From a psychodynamic orientation to a structural family therapy approach in the treatment of drug dependency. In E. Kaufman & P. Kaufmann (Eds.), *Family Ther-*

apy of Drug and Alcohol Abuse. New York: Gardner Press, 1979, 43–54.

Khantzian, E. An ego/self theory of substance dependence: A contemporary psychoanalytic perspective. In D.J. Letteiri (Ed.), M. Sayers, & H.W. Pearson (Eds.), *Theories on drug abuse: Selected contemporary perspectives.* Rockville, Md.: National Institute on Drug Abuse Research Monograph 30, March 1980, 29–33.

Khantzian, E.J. Psychopathology, psychodynamics and alcoholism. In E.M. Pattison, & E. Kaufman (Eds.), *Encyclopedia Handbook of Psychiatry.* New York: Gardner Press, 1982, 581–597.

Kreek, M.J. Physiologic implications of methadone treatment. In *Proceedings of the 5th National Conference on Methadone Treatment.* New York: National Association for the Prevention of Addiction to Narcotics, 1973, 824–835.

Lachar, D., Berman, W., Grisell, J.L. and Schoof, K. A heroin addiction scale for the MMPI: Effectiveness in differential diagnosis in a psychiatric setting. *International Journal of Addiction,* 1979, *14,* 135–142.

MacAndrew, C. The differentiation of male alcoholic outpatients by means of the MMPI. *Quarterly Journal of Studies of Alcoholism,* 1965, *26,* 238–246.

Milkman, H., & Frosch, W. Theory of drug use. In D.J. Lettieri, M. Sayers, & H.W. Pearson (Eds), *Theories on drug abuse: Selected contemporary perspectives.* Rockville, Md.: National Institute on Drug Abuse Research Monograph 30, March 1980.

Milkman, H., & Frosch, W. On the preferential abuse of heroin and amphetamine, *Journal of Nervous Mental Disorders,* 1973, *156*(4), 242–248.

National Institute of Alcohol and Alcohol Abuse, Information and Feature Service, ADAMHA, December 1, 1982, p. 1.

Pattison, E.M., & Kaufman, E. Alcoholism syndrome, definition and models. In *Encyclopedic handbook of alcoholism.* Pattison E.M., Kaufman, E. (Eds.), New York: Gardner, Press, 1982, 3–30.

Rado, S. The psychic effects of intoxicants: An attempt to evolve a psychoanalytical theory of morbid cravings. In S. Rado (Ed.), *Psychoanalysis of behavior.* New York: Grune and Stratton, 1956, 25–39.

Richman, A. Trends in the use of multiple drugs by narcotic addicts, 1972–1975. In *Proceedings of the 2nd National Drug Abuse Conference, New Orleans, La., April 4–7, 1975.* New York: Marcel Dekker, 1976.

Rosen, A., Ottenberg, D.J., & Barr, J.L. Patterns of previous use of alcohol in a group of hospitalized drug addicts. *Drug Forum*, 1975, 4(3), 261–272.

Rosenberger, C.M. Young alcoholics. *British Journal of Psychiatry*, 1969, *115*, 181–188.

Sandmaier, M. *The invisible alcoholics*. New York: McGraw Hill, 1980.

Santo, Y., Farley, E.C., & Friedman, A.S. Highlights from the national youth polydrug study. In *Drug abuse patterns among polydrug users and urban appalachian youths*. Department of Health, Education and Welfare, 1980, 1–16.

Schnoll, S.H. *Alcohol and other substance abuse in adolescents in addiction research and treatment: Converging trends*. New York: Pergamon Press, 1979.

Schuckit, M.A. Combined alcohol and drug abuse. *Advances in Alcoholism*, 1973, *34*, 1356–1359.

Schuckit, M., Pitts, F.N., Reich, T. Alcoholism: Two types of alcoholism in women. *Archives of General Psychiatry*, 1969, *20*(3), 301–306.

Schut, J., File, K., & Wohlmuth, T. Alcohol use by narcotic addicts in methadone maintenance treatment. *Quarterly Journal of Studies in Alcohol*, 1973, *34*, 1356–1359.

Stimmel, B., Cohen, M., & Hanbury, R. Alcoholism and polydrug abuse in persons in methadone maintenance. *Annals of the New York Academy of Science*, 1978, *311*, 99–109.

Spotts, J.V., & Shontz, F.C. A life-time theory of chronic drug abuse in theories on drug abuse. In D.J. Lettieri, M. Sayers, & H.W. Pearson (Eds.), *Theories on drug abuse: Selected contemporary perspectives*. Rockville, Md.: NIDA Research Monograph 30, March, 1980.

Tuckfield, B.S., McLeroy, K.R., Waterhose, G.J. *Multiple drug use among persons with alcohol related problems*. Research Triangle Park, N.C.: Research Triangle Institute, 1975.

Vaillant, G.E. Natural history of male psychological health. Antecedents of Alcoholism and "Morality." *American Journal of Psychiatry*, 1980, *37*(2), 181–186.

Wechsler, H., & Thum, D. Teenage drinking, drug use and social correlates. *Quarterly Journal of Studies on Alcohol*, 1973, *34*, 1220–1227.

Weisman, M.M., Meyers, J.K., & Harding, P.S. The prevalence rates and psychiatric heterogeneity of alcoholism in a United States urban community. *Quarterly Journal of Studies on Alcoholism*, 1980, 672–681.

Wesson, D.R., Carlin, A.S., Adams, K.M., & Beschner, G. *Polydrug abuse: The results of a national collaborative study.* New York: Academic Press, 1978.

Winokur, G., Reich, T., Rimmer, J. Alcoholism. III. Diagnosis and familial psychiatric illness in 259 alcoholic probands. *Archives of General Psychiatry,* 1970, *23,* 104–111.

Woodruff, R.A., Guze, S.B., Clayton, P.J., & Carr, I. Alcoholism and depression. *Archives of General Psychiatry,* 1973, *29,* 97–100.

Wurmser, L. *Drug use as a protective system.* in D.J. Lettieri, M. Sayers, & H.W. Pearson (Eds.), *Theories on drug abuse: Selected contemporary perspectives.* Rockville, Md.: NIDA Research Monograph 30, March 1980, 71–74.

Part II

FAMILY SYSTEMS

Chapter 2

Family Systems
of Adult Male Alcoholics
and Alcohol Abusers

Until very recently, the literature in the field of alcoholism has generally ignored family dynamics (Orford, Oppenheimer, Egert, Hermann, & Gutline, 1976). At the same time, the family therapy literature was also almost totally devoid of consideration of alcoholism (Pattison & Kaufman, 1981). However, after years of neglect, research into the alcoholic family has "come of age" (Steinglass, 1980) in the utilization of family systems research techniques in the study of alcoholism.

Family systems of adult male alcoholics are presented as separate from those seen of drug abusers because the bulk of studies in this field, including my own earlier studies, have been conducted separately. However, the reader should bear in mind that frequently we are describing the same families in both cases, although we may be viewing them from different generations or at different stages of their family life cycles. In this chapter we will use primarily the male gender when referring to the alcoholic.

FAMILY SYSTEMS

Some family interactional patterns are unique to alcoholism and some are seen in other neurotic families. On the basis of clinical experience, Pattison and Kaufman (1981) divided

29

alcoholic families into four subgroups, each with a distinctive family pattern.

The Functional Family System
(The Family with an Alcoholic Member)

These family systems appear to be stabilized and happy. The parents maintain a loving spousal relationship and a relatively good sexual adjustment. They are successful as a parenting team. Their children are well adjusted and have good relationships with each other as well as with their peers.

These families have learned to function with a minimum of overt conflict. They may be sensitive to social standards and values and respond to social authorities (ministers, physicians, supervisors). Although such families function well and are responsive to external change, they are usually resistant to internal change.

The emotional balance of the family is likely to be positive, with a desire to retain and rehabilitate the alcoholic member (Kaufman & Pattison, 1981). Because of the lack of obvious conflict and the general good family function, the focus of family concern is likely to be on the alcoholic member. The alcoholism does not evolve as a result of family stresses but primarily in response to social strains and/or personal neurotic conflict. Excessive drinking is often done outside the home. This type of family system usually exists in the early phases of alcoholism and may deteriorate in later stages. Steinglass (1980) also recognized this type of alcoholic family, stating that they function by walling off, and isolating the alcoholic behavior. He called such families "stable-wet."

The Neurotic Enmeshed Family System
(The Alcoholic Family)

In these families, alcohol use plays a critical role in daily behavior and is a central organizing principal around which most interactions are focused (Steinglass, 1980). Drinking behavior interrupts normal family tasks, causes conflict, shifts roles, and demands adjustive and adaptive responses from family members who do not know how to appropriately respond. A converse dynamic also occurs: marital and family styles, rules, and conflict may evoke, support, and maintain alcoholism as a symptom of family system dysfunction or as a coping mechanism to deal with family anxiety. These family systems are the ones most frequently described in the alcoholism literature and will be described in detail later in this chapter.

The Disintegrated Family System
(The Separated Family)

In this system there is a past history of reasonable vocational function and family life, followed by a progressive deterioration that may include loss of job, loss of self-respect, family instability, inability to function in the family, and, finally, separation from the family. The family may become destitute and turn to inlaws or welfare. The alcoholic is now totally alienated from the nuclear family and inlaws, but may retain ties to the family of origin. The alcoholic usually presents to a hospital or clinic without any family, and frequently without any recent family contact. Usually he requires immediate physical support in terms of room, food, and clothes, and is usually without the necessary resources to return to independent function. The families of such individuals usually cannot and will not reconstitute during the early phases of alcoholism rehabilitation. Thus, the initial and early stages of treatment should focus primarily on the individual alcoholic. However, potential ties to spouse, family, kin, and friends should be explored early in treatment and some contact should be initiated, although there should be neither explicit or implicit assumptions that family ties will be fully reconstituted. When several months of sobriety and personal stability have been achieved, more substantive family explorations can be initiated to re-establish parental roles and family and kinship relations.

The Absent Family System
(The Longterm Isolated Alcoholic)

Although this system may be found in end-stage alcoholism, more often it is marked by total loss of family of origin early in the drinking career. Such persons usually have never married or have had only brief relationships. They may have relatives or inlaws with whom they maintain perfunctory contact. These persons rarely have close friendships, and have minimal social or vocational skills. Their significant others are usually boarding home operators or buddies who chip in to buy a bottle of cheap wine. Since the vast majority have never acquired adequate life skills, the goal is *not* rehabilitation. These alcoholics do best in partially institutionalized social support systems (Kaufman & Pattison, 1981).

THE FAMILY SYSTEM AND ALCOHOLISM

The Effect of Alcoholism on the Family

Regardless of the type of family system, alcoholism is a major stress on the family. It is an economic drain on family resources, threatens job security, interrupts normal family tasks, causes conflict, and demands adjustive, adaptive responses from family members who do not know how to appropriately respond. In brief, alcoholism creates a series of escalating crises in family structure and function, which may bring the family system to an extreme crisis. In addition to these psychological consequences, alcoholism creates physical problems, most notably sexual impotence or dysfunction, which in turn produces further marital conflict (Pattison & Kaufman, 1981).

The Effect of the Family on Alcoholism

A converse dynamic also occurs, in that marital and family conflict may evoke, support, and maintain alcoholism as a *symptom* of family system dysfunction, as a coping *mechanism* to deal with family dysfunction, and as a *consequence* of dysfunctional family styles, rules, and patterns of alcohol use. Therefore, alcoholism is both the cause and the *effect* of family dysfunction (Pattison & Kaufman, 1981).

Early studies focused on the personality structures of husbands and wives, assuming that conflicts based on individual differences were the basic problem (Ballard, 1959). Most studies focused on the male alcoholic and his non-alcoholic wife. It was often implied that the wife was neurotic and chose an alcoholic husband, or that the wife became neurotic because of her husband's alcoholism. Perhaps even more misogynist was the view that the wife "drove her husband to drink." In retrospect, these studies, which focused primarily on personality, were marred by selective biased samples, lack of comparative controls, and reductionistic interpretations of psychodynamics as psychopathology (Fox, 1956). Thus, I feel that the fable of the noxious wife is just that—a fable (Kogan & Jackson, 1965). Thus, there is no validity to the descriptions of "typical wives of alcoholics," nor can one even conclude that wives of alcoholics are somehow different from other wives. The same problems pertain to the study of men who marry women alcoholics. Although there are few studies, these reports often indicate significant psychopathology among these men. However, better samples and comparative data may likewise demonstrate no specific type of male spouse of alcoholic women (Rimmer, 1974).

It is more useful to study the marital interactional dynamics, role perceptions, and patterns of expectations and sanctions about the use of alcohol. Couples with alcoholism engage in neurotic interactional behavior which at times is similar to behavior seen in other neurotic marriages, both of which are dissimilar from healthy marital interaction. However, alcoholic marriages also have certain unique characteristics, which are essential to their understanding and treatment. One finding that differentiates alcoholic (and drug-abusing) families from other families is the high incidence of alcoholism in the families of origin of both the alcoholic and the spouse. Vaillant (1983) has suggested that the severely disturbed family environment, which leads to alcoholism in progeny, may result from parental alcoholism more than from any other single familial factor. Quantitative studies of communication patterns have demonstrated several specific abnormalities in the families of alcoholics. Gorad (1971) has shown that male alcoholics exceed their wives, normal husbands, and normal wives in the use of responsibility-avoiding messages. Gorad also found that both the alcoholic and his wife are highly competitive in style, using "one up" messages more and cooperating less than other couples.

Jacob, Ridney, Evitkovic, and Blane (1981) studied alcoholic families both sober and under the influence of alcohol, and compared them to non-alcoholic controls. They found that in alcoholic families spousal interactions had more negative affect, that the negative affect increased in the presence of alcohol, and that alcoholic fathers showed less leadership, assertiveness, and problem-solving behavior with spouse and children. Orford et al. (1976) found that, particularly in those alcoholic families with a poor prognosis, wives gave and received little affection, used few socially desirable adjectives in describing their "sober" husbands, and expected their husbands to use "hostile-dominance" adjectives or phrases. Chiles, Strauss, and Benjamin (1980) compared four alcoholic couples with sexual dysfunction with a control group of non-alcoholic couples with sexual dysfunction. They did not find significant differences in wives' dominance as described by either husbands or wives. However, alcoholic husbands saw themselves as most submissive of the four partners, although their wives disagreed. Chiles et al. suggested that male alcoholics feel submissive because of their own need to misperceive the situation, not because their wives are dominant and force them into submission.

Gorad (1971) also noted that the alcoholic's wife appears dominating because she is responsible and direct, but that she is unable to control her husband and that neither spouse accepts that the other will ever change. Paolino and McCrady (1979), noted that these "couples blame each other, put each other down, turn each other off and compete for dominance. They sidetrack each other, do not come up with solutions and then terminate communication, leading to the alcoholic's fleeing the scene to drink." Olson (1982) studied 300 "chemically dependent families" with FACES I (Family Adaptability and Cohesion Evaluation Scale) and has found more of them to be "chaotically disengaged" than controls. He noted little difference in extremes in the enmeshed dimension. In my own pilot studies of 26 alcoholic families I found that the mean scores on FACES I were surprisingly within normal limits. When the scores were viewed by separating out pathologic families, about a fourth of alcoholics viewed the family as disengaged (23 percent), as compared to 29 percent in Olson's study. However, the other family members viewed the family as chaotic in 19 percent of my families (Olson: 24 percent) and rigid in 19 percent of cases (Olson: 13 percent) but disengaged in only 6 percent of cases (Olson: 32 percent). Using the family APGAR* (Smilkstein, 1978) with my same 26 families, 10 identified patients viewed the family as dysfunctional, and 16 of the families' overall ratings were dysfunctional. Both Olson's findings and my own are in contrast to most descriptive studies, which describe the alcoholic's family as highly reactive and enmeshed. This may be due to reactive disengagement in the later phases of alcoholism.

THE FAMILY AND ALCOHOLISM AS A RECIPROCAL EXTENDED FAMILY SYSTEMS PROBLEM

Recent family research has moved away from a focus on the marital partners toward a consideration of the family system, the families of origin, the lifestyles of children from alcoholic families, and the kin structures of the extended family system. This provides a much broader view of alcoholism as a family problem.

Experimental observations of family systems show that alcohol use in a family is not just an individual matter. The use of alcohol and the consequential behavior of drinking is dynamically related to events in the family system. Thus, the use of alcohol is *purposeful, adaptive, homeostatic,* and *meaningful.* The problem of alcoholism is not just the consequences of drinking per se, but more importantly, the *system functions* that are filled by drinking in the dynamics of the family system (Davis, Berenson, Steinglass, & Davis, 1974; Steinglass, Winer, & Mandelson, 1971).

We can extend the systems approach to a larger consideration of the nuclear family embedded in generational and extended family systems. The problem of alcoholism runs in families, across generations, and into the kinship system. However, alcoholism may also be idiosyncratic to an individual per-

---

*APGAR: measures Adaptation, Partnership, Growth, Affection, and Resolve

son. Cotton (1979) showed that different studies report no familial alcoholism in 47 to 82 percent of cases. On the other hand, he reported that 33 percent of alcoholics have a parent who is alcoholic, and in 82 percent of cases a member of the extended family system has alcoholism.

Alcoholism has been thought to be a genetic syndrome (Goodwin, 1976). While genetics may determine differences in metabolic and physiologic responses, and thus, contribute to the vulnerability to alcohol abuse, genetic differences seem implausible as the major determinant of the behaviors related to alcoholism. On the other hand, recent studies have carefully delineated the psychological transmission of alcohol abuse patterns from parents to children in several generations (Hoffman & Noem, 1975; Wolin, Bennett, & Noonan, 1979) and similar patterns of vulnerability to alcoholism based on interactional experience with alcoholic parents (Rimmer & Winokur, 1972). Thus, alcoholism may not be just an individual problem, nor a problem of marital partners, nor a problem of the nuclear family system, but may reflect larger alcoholism-generating family systems.

CHILDREN IN THE ALCOHOLIC FAMILY SYSTEM

Much of the early alcoholism family literature focused primarily on the marital partners, neglecting the roles and functions of children in the family and the consequences of alcoholism for the children. Margaret Cork (1969) named them "The forgotten children." In the alcoholic family, children are often the most severely victimized. They have growth and development problems, school and learning problems, emotional problems, and, frequently, significant behavior dysfunctions (El-Guebaly & Orford, 1977). Further, they are often subject to gross neglect and abuse. (Teenage children are not immune to these adverse consequences, even though they are often considered less vulnerable.) Just as significant are the longterm adverse consequences on personality patterning, identity formation, and attitudes toward alcohol. Many children of alcoholics become overly concerned with taking care of others. Family intervention must truly consider the needs of the children, in terms of both short-range problems and longer-term preventive concerns (Pattison & Kaufman, 1981).

Children must also be considered producers and perpetuators of family dysfunction, depending on their family role. For example, a latency-age child may encourage a parent to drink to quiet the violence or to loosen controls to a point where affection is shown. A teenager may provoke a cycle of drinking and fighting with his or her parents so that they will be unable to set limits and enforce punishments. Vice versa, alcoholic parents may use their children's behavior problems as excuses to drink.

The family system of a teenage alcoholic will be virtually identical to that of a same-age drug abuser, all other factors being equal.

TYPICAL FAMILY SYSTEMS AND DYNAMICS*

Like most symptoms of family dysfunction, alcoholism is a systems-maintaining and a systems-maintained device. Drinking may be a symptom or an expression of stress created by conflicts within the family system. Excessive drinking usually occurs when family anxiety is high, but drinking stirs up higher anxiety in those dependent on the one who drinks. The anxiety causes everyone to do more of what they are already doing. Drinking to relieve anxiety and increased family anxiety in response to drinking can spiral into a crisis, lead to collapse, or establish a chronic pattern (Bowen, 1974). Drinking frequently triggers anger in the drinker and provocation in others, which then triggers further anger and provocation despite attempts by the alcoholic to absorb the anger with alcohol. Drinking contributes significantly to provocation, verbal abuse, and physical violence. Drunkenness is important to communication

---

*This section deals primarily with the neurotic enmeshed family system.

problems. Communication with a drunk is frustrating and exasperating and frequently leads to anger.

In triangulating family systems, conflict or distance between two parties is automatically displaced onto a third party (e.g., inlaw, lover, therapist, child), issue, or substance (alcohol or drugs) (Bowen, 1974). This is in contrast to a threesome in which each member can interact freely with the other two and without interference. Triangulating family systems are prone to alcoholism.

Individuals tend to choose spouses with equal levels of ego strength and self-awareness but with opposite ways of dealing with stress. We see frequently that opposites attract. Obsessives, particularly, are attracted to hysterics. In such relationships each person sees him- or herself as giving in to the other. The one who gives in the most becomes "de-selfed" and is vulnerable to a drinking problem (Bowen, 1974). If it is the husband, he becomes more and more burdened by his responsibility to his job, wife, and children. Consequently he increases his social drinking, particularly at home, but manages to prolong his functioning at work for many years. Even after a pattern of alcoholism is established, these couples continue indefinitely in a highly competitive relationship, with neither partner becoming clearly dominant. Fighting frequently occurs in regard to each partner blaming the other for the family's problems. This dual projection blinds the couple from seeing their respective roles in creating problems. They frequently fight endlessly about "who started it" and readily duplicate this position in therapy, hoping that the therapist will judge right and wrong. Another frequent pattern is to let the drunk person set the rules, follow his or her lead, cease trying to communicate, and withdraw. Withdrawal involves long periods of silence and, in the long run, leads to escalation of negative feelings and distrust and, ultimately, to explosive expressions of anger.

The male alcoholic leaves his spouse starved for attention and affection. Early in the marriage, he expresses love through sex and material possessions. Since the alcoholic believes that sex forgives all transgressions, particularly drinking, the spouse then withholds affection because it leads to sex and thus to forgiveness. As alcoholism progresses, the alcoholic becomes more unable to perform sexually, and the marriage becomes asexual. The alcoholic loses the spousal role in other areas as well. He readily gives up his role as parent. Other roles, such as household chores and maintenance, are also rapidly abandoned. The breadwinner function is the last to go, and job loss may be necessary before treatment is sought. Alcoholic fathers are prone to abuse their children through beatings or sexual assaults.

Co-alcoholism

The non-alcoholic wife may encourage the oldest son to take over responsibilities abdicated by the father, placing the son in overt competition with his father. As non-alcoholic members take over full management of the family, the alcoholic is relegated to child status, which perpetuates drinking. Coalitions occur between the non-alcoholic spouse and children or inlaws, which tend to further distance the alcoholic. Children are terrified of the violence so commonly seen in alcoholic families, and school phobia may result from the child's desire to stay home to protect the parent(s) from harm. These families develop a chronic atmosphere of silence and tension, and their children complain of a lack of fun and laughter.

The non-alcoholic wife may neglect her children because she is directing her attention to the alcoholic. Although not all alcoholics seriously abuse or neglect their children, the majority have difficulties in child-rearing. The emotional disturbances that characterize alcoholic families leave the children feeling rejected and unable to identify with either parent (Pattison & Kaufman, 1981).

The patterns that develop in non-alcoholic family members have been labeled *co-alcoholism*. The early phases of co-alcoholism involve denial, rationalization, and the hope that the alcoholic's behavior will improve. There is a feeling of responsibility and guilt for the alcoholic's behavior, and some withdrawal. In the middle phases. hostility, disgust, pity, and protectiveness and shielding of the alcoholic are common. The co-alcoholic frequently drinks with the alcoholic as a way of tolerating his behavior. In the advanced stages, hostility, withdrawal, and suspiciousness become generalized to the total environment. In the final stages of co-alcoholism, responsibility for and quarrelling with the alcoholic are all-encompassing. Outside interests decline, and needs to maintain the self are disregarded. Psychosomatic symptoms or drug and alcohol dependence may occur, and separation is threatened or demanded. Frequently, the alcoholic will become sufficiently motivated for treatment when the co-alcoholic reaches the detachment aspects of these final phases.

Wiseman (1980) has described the wife's attempt to deal with an alcoholic husband as "home treatment" in which she uses a series of strategies depending on the stage of her relationship to her husband and the failure of previous strategies. The 76 wives Wiseman studied began with direct approaches, including logical persuasion, nagging, emotional pleading, and threats to leave. When the direct approaches failed, they then resorted to indirect methods, including acting normal and uninvolved, preventing anything that could upset the alcoholic, and, finally (often with the help of Al-Anon), taking a totally hands-off approach.

Moos, Finney, and Gamble (1982) conducted a study of alcoholics and their spouses compared to a matched control group. They found the following characteristics in the spouses of alcoholics: more alcohol consumption, more negative life events, fewer social and recreational activities, less family cohesiveness, more depression, more medical conditions, and more job changes. They also noted that when the alcoholic controlled his drinking, the negative effects on the spouse diminished.

Co-alcoholism is so painful and symptomatic that specific programs have been developed for its treatment.

The Impact of Sobriety on the Family System

The spouse and family build up many defenses which create problems when and if the alcoholic gets sober. If the alcoholic stops drinking, the spouse no longer fights with him or her about active drinking but about whether he or she will *resume* drinking, which paradoxically triggers resumption of drinking.

The grief work involved in giving up alcohol may last for months or years. During this period of prolonged grief and high, unfulfilled expectations, the recovering alcoholic is referred to as a "dry drunk." A dry drunk is an alcoholic who has stopped drinking but who continues his unreasonable and manipulative behavior. Characteristically, he punishes others because he expects but does not receive exceptional rewards for not drinking. If the family system is not worked with during this phase of the cycle, and if the family does not learn new patterns of relating to each other to replace those developed during alcoholism, then the slightest stress will cause the alcoholic to return to symptomatic consumption of alcohol and the family members will regress as well.

These observations emphasize the importance of family therapy to the ultimate benefit of the total system. What has frequently been neglected is the importance of involving the total family (children, parents, and inlaws) in therapy to ameliorate or stop the drinking. What is seen most commonly is a family system in which the non-alcoholic parent has made a cross-generational coalition with a child, generally of the opposite sex, which excludes, alienates, and infantilizes the alcoholic. Such coalitions are also common between the co-alcoholic and her own parents or a lover, or between the alcoholic and a lover (frequently also from an alcoholic family). Thus, attention to familial relationships outside of the alcoholic–spouse dyad are essential to understanding and changing the alcoholic as well as maintaining sobriety.

The Family as a Determinant of Rehabilitation

Alcoholic families have developed a homeostatic adjustment to years of substance abuse. When the alcoholic returns, the force of that homeostasis will tend to draw the alcoholic and family back to their old patterns. The alcoholic may be instantly demanding of his pre–substance-abuse role as well as expecting inordinate rewards and recognition for giving up alcohol. The family members are waiting for longterm changes and are unwilling to give up the roles and alliances they developed during the period of co-alcoholism. The duration and intensity of these roles and systems are so powerful that family intervention may have to be intense as well as longterm (3–12 months), with follow-up sessions extended over several years. Moreover a return of tension and dysfunction may result if the entire family is not worked with for the necessary amount of time.

In keeping with the observations of alcoholism as a systems problem, the attitudes, structure, and function of the family system have been shown to be extremely important in the successful outcome of alcoholism treatment. The alcoholic person enters treatment from a family system and usually returns to that family system. If the system is dysfunctional it may vitiate any individual treatment gains. If the family changes or adopts more appropriate functions, it will sustain improvement and change in the alcoholic member (Moos, Bromet, Tsu, & Moos, 1979; Rae, 1972).

—————————————————————————————— REFERENCES

Ballard, R.G. The interaction between marital conflict and alcoholism as seen through MMPI's of marriage partners. *American Journal of Orthopsychiatry*, 1959, *29*, 528–546.

Bowen, M. Alcoholism as viewed through family systems theory and family psychotherapy. *Annals of the New York Academy of Science*, 1974, *233*, 115–122.

Chiles, J.A., Strauss, F.S., & Benjamin, L.S. Marital conflict and sexual dysfunction in alcoholic and nonalcoholic couples. *British Journal of Psychiatry*, 1980, *137*, 266–273.

Cork, M.R. *The forgotten children.* Toronto: Addict Research Foundation, 1969.

Cotton, N.S. The familial incidence of alcoholism: A review. *Journal of the Studies of Alcohol*, 1979, *40*, 89–116.

Davis, D., Berenson, D., Steinglass, P., & Davis, S. The adaptive consequences of drinking. *Psychiatry*, 1974, *37*, 209–215.

El-Guebaly, N., & Orford, D.R. The offspring of alcoholics: A critical review. *American Journal of Psychiatry*, 1977, *134*, 357–365.

Fox, R. The alcoholic spouse. In Eisenstein, V.M., (Ed.): *Neurotic interaction in marriage.* New York: Basic Books, 1956.

Goodwin, D.W. *Is alcoholism hereditary?* New York: Oxford University Press, 1976.

Gorad, S.L. Communicational styles and interaction of alcoholics and their wives. *Family Process*, 1971, *10*, 475–489.

Hoffman, N. & Noem, A.A. Alcoholism among parents of male and female alcoholics. *Psychology Reports*, 1975, *36*, 322–323.

Jacob, T., Richey, D., Evitkovic, J.F., & Blane, H.T. Communications styles of alcoholic and nonalcoholic families when drinking and not drinking. *Journal of Studies on Alcohol*, 1981, *42*(5), 466–482.

Kaufman, E., & Pattison, E.M. Differential methods of family therapy in the treatment of alcoholism. *Journal of Studies on Alcohol*, 1981, *42*(11), 951–971.

Kogan, K.L., & Jackson, J.K. Some concomitants of personal difficulties in wives of alcoholics and nonalcoholics. *Quarterly Journal of Studies on Alcohol*, 1965, *26*, 595–604.

Moos, R.H., Bromet, E., Tsu, V., & Moos, B. Family characteristics and the outcome of treatment of alcoholics. *Journal of Studies on Alcohol*, 1979, *40*, 78–88.

Moos, R.H., Finney, J.W., & Gamble, W. The process of recovery from alcoholism. II. Comparing spouses of alcoholic patients and matched community controls. *Journal of Studies on Alcohol*, 1982, *3*(9), 888–909.

Olson, D. Personal Communication, 1982.

Orford, J., Oppenheimer, E., Egert, S., Herrman, C., & Gutline, S. The cohesiveness of alcoholism-complicated marriage and its influence on treatment outcome. *British Journal of Psychiatry*, 1976, *128*, 318–319.

Paolino, T.J., Jr., & McCrady, B.S. *The alcoholic marriage: Alternative perspectives*. New York: Grune & Stratton, 1979.

Pattison, E.M., & Kaufman, E. Family therapy in the treatment of alcoholism. In M.R. Langsley (Ed.), *Family therapy and margin psychopathology*. New York: Grune & Stratton, 1981, 203–230.

Rae, J.B. The influence of wives on the treatment outcome of alcoholics: A followup study of two years. *British Journal of Psychiatry*, 1972, *120*, 601–613.

Rimmer, J. Psychiatric illness in husbands of alcoholics. *Quarterly Journal of Studies on Alcohol*, 1974, *35*, 281–283.

Smilkstein, G. The family APGAR: A proposal for a family function test and its use by physicians. *The Journal of Family Practice*, 1978, *6*, 1231–1239.

Steinglass, P. A life history model of the alcoholic. *Family Process*, 1980, *19*, 211–226.

Steinglass, P., Winer, S., & Mandelson, J.H. A systems approach to alcoholism: A model and its clinical application. *Archives of General Psychiatry*, 1971, *24*, 401–408.

Wiseman, J.P. The "home treatment": The first steps in trying to cope with an alcoholic husband. *Family Relations,* 1980, *29,* 541–549.

Wolin, S.J., Bennett, L.A., & Noonan, D.L. Family rituals and the recurrence of alcoholism over generations. *American Journal of Psychiatry,* 1979, *136,* 589–593.

Chapter 3

Family Systems of Male Drug-Abusing and Drug-Dependent Individuals

There is no one family pattern that is specific to all drug abusers or all drug addicts. However, there are overall trends, some of which predate the onset of substance abuse and some of which are the result of drug abuse. Familiarity with these family systems and reaction patterns is essential to the family therapist who works with these families. It is particularly important that the therapist not apply knowledge of patterns to families before observing them but uses this knowledge to enhance sensitivity and understanding.

Although many of these family systems and reactions apply to females, this chapter will deal primarily with males. Therefore I will use primarily the male gender pronouns when discussing nonspecific persons in this chapter. The unique aspects of the families of female drug abusers will be dealt with in Chapter 4.

ADOLESCENT SUBSTANCE ABUSE

Family Reactivity

Adolescents frequently abuse drugs and alcohol as part of problems with socialization and nonconformity. Generally, the

45

children first become seriously vulnerable to substance abuse upon entering junior high school. Drug-abusing adolescents may refuse to follow parental rules for behavior at home (Hendin, Pollinger, Ulman, & Carr, 1981). They consistently object to doing household chores, and when they do them they often disappear before completion, particularly if they have already been paid for the job or received their allowance. They associate with and bring home individuals whom their parents consider a bad influence. Yet, when damage is done to the house they blame their friends, although they never seem to know which one specifically committed the act. They come home later than expected and without calling, which infuriates their parents (Hendin et al., 1981). They drive the family car without permission to locations that are off limits. They frequently get traffic citations that they can't afford to pay and that require parental court appearances. They are constantly in trouble at school, particularly through tardiness, absence, not paying attention, and unruly behavior, yet they develop many ways of intercepting messages from school to parents. Shoplifting, theft from and damages to friends' homes are also common. They lie to their parents about needing funds, which are diverted to drugs. When this is discovered, they are coerced by threats of violence from debtors, commission of crimes, and protection from incarceration to continue to provide monies for drugs. These adolescents continue to drink and use drugs at home after they've been prohibited from doing so, even with legal reinforcement. They lie about their substance abuse and destructive behavior, and the lies themselves frequently become a major concern to parents. They also engage their parents in frequent power struggles about whether they are high or have used drugs.

This kind of behavior leads many parents to feel they have totally lost control of their children. Some parents respond by attempting to totally abdegate responsibility but find it impossible to remain detached because the adolescent still manages to draw them into their problematic behavior even after they move out of the house. Other parents respond by becoming extremely controlling and limiting, at times to a point where the child is totally restricted and has lost all privileges (Hendin et al. 1981). The child then still manages to act out and the parents feel powerless because they feel they have no means left to enforce structure and control. At such times parents may resort to physical brutality and violence, which only serves to escalate defiance, substance abuse, and other self-destructive behaviors. In these cases, parents frequently become totally preoccupied with the adolescent's behavior and their inability to contain it, causing themselves a great deal of suffering. Concern for their child may create distance between the spouses. Such distance may function as a needed buffer or may create painful sexual and emotional withdrawal. Many of these patterns are seen in families with defiant or antisocial adolescents, even when there is no substance abuse. However, these patterns of family interaction are rare without some drug or alcohol abuse, as this abuse is commonly a part of teenage defiance and causes cycles of increasingly antisocial behavior.

In some families the adolescent's drug use and other problems may be denied for years, even in the face of overwhelming evidence. Even these heavily denying families may shift to over-involvement when the drug abuse is discovered.

Family Reactions to Adolescent Substance Abuse

The family system frequently revolves around the drug abuser as a scapegoat upon whom all problems are focused. Often, the family's basic interactional pattern is dull and lifeless and only becomes lively when mobilized to deal with the crises of drug abuse (Reilly, 1976). At times the adolescent's difficulties may be an attempt to keep combative parents together or to reunite separated parents. Guilt is a frequent currency of manipulation. It may be used by the drug abuser to coerce the family into continued financial and emotional support of drug use, or by parents to curb individuation (Kaufman & Kaufmann, 1979). Many mothers have severe depression, anxiety, or psychosomatic symptoms that are blamed on the drug abuser, thereby reinforcing the pattern of guilt and mutual manipulation. Maternal drug and alcohol abuse and suicide attempts may also be blamed on the drug abuser.

Physical expressions of love and affection are frequently absent or used to deny and obliterate individuation or conflict.

Anger about interpersonal conflicts is not expressed directly unless it erupts in explosive violence. Anger about drug use and denial of it is expressed quite frequently and is almost always counterproductive. Everyone's life is taken up with the sufferings and entanglements of the substance-abusing child. However, in many cases, the joylessness preceded the addiction. As Reilly (1976) noted, communication is most frequently negative and there is no appropriate praise for good behavior. There is a lack of consistent limit-setting by parents, so that the same behavior may be punished or rewarded at different times (Fort, 1954).

Adolescent drug abuse is frequently an expression of defiance which actually leads to infantilization and continuing intense family ties, albeit conflictual ones. These families frequently undergo pseudoindividuation through institutionalization, runaways with crises which result in brief reunions, and scrapes with authorities that result in incarceration or parental bailout. Thus, though the drug-abusing adolescent may be hundreds of miles from home, his behavior continues to deeply affect and be affected by parental ties.

Families of Heroin Addicts

I conducted a four-year study of the families of 78 heroin-abusing and heroin-dependent youths from 75 families in New York City and Los Angeles. Each family was treated for about six months (Kaufman & Kaufmann, 1979; Kaufman, 1981). Most observers of the families of hard-core drug abusers have noted several consistent themes, which were either confirmed or clarified by my study. My findings approximated those of families in which abuse of "softer" drugs (e.g., marijuana, alcohol) is the presenting problem, although problems with soft drugs are frequently less intense. In these 75 families, 88 percent of the mothers were emotionally enmeshed with their drug-abusing children, (mainly sons) to the extent that their emotional state was totally dependent on the behavior of and closeness with these children. Although 43 percent of fathers were absent or emotionally disengaged from the entire family, 41 percent were enmeshed with the drug abuser as well as the rest of the family. The relatively high percentage of enmeshed fathers in this study includes those who were overinvolved with female hard-core drug abusing daughters and those who stayed enmeshed in Italian and Jewish families. (Italian and Jewish families were more highly represented in my sample than in other similar studies.)

Sibling Importance

The role of siblings of drug abusers has also been consistently overlooked. Siblings tend to fall equally into two basic categories: very good and very bad. The "bad" group is composed of fellow drug abusers whose drug use is inextricably fused with that of the identified patient (IP). The "good" group includes children who assume the role of an authoritarian parent when the father is absent or disengaged and/or are highly successful in their own careers. Some of these successful siblings had individuated from the family, but many were still enmeshed. Hendin, Pollinger, Ulman & Carr (1981) noted that drug-free siblings were frequently "good" even before drug use began and that this dichotomy contributes to the difficulties of the IP. Another small group of "good" siblings in my sample were quite passive and not involved with substance abuse. Some of these developed disorders such as depression, tics and headaches, which are related to retroflexing anger. Cleveland (1981) noted that the "good" child in these families obeys family rules and works hard in school, attempting to meet their parents' high expectations. They bear the burden of the IP and their "incompetent" parents. They feel if they can only be good enough they will erase the effect of the IP and make their parents look good. "Good" children are rigid, lonely, and suffer guilt and remorse, often for the rest of their lives. On the other hand, enmeshed drug-abusing siblings may provide drugs for each other, inject drugs into one another, set each other up to be arrested, or even pimp for one another. At times, a large family may show both types of sibling relationships. Many successful older siblings in my study were quite successful throughout their lives. In these cases, the younger patient sibling withdrew from any vocational achievement rather than compete in a situation where they had little chance for success as compared to their older siblings.

In a few cases drug abusers I studied were themselves parental children who had no way of asking for relief of responsibility except through drugs. More commonly, they were the youngest child—and their drug abuse maintained their role as the baby. They were frequently the child who gets the most attention, and drug abuse kept them from ever having to abandon the parental nest, serving an important function for parents who needed to have chidren around to focus on.

Family Enmeshment

The extent of enmeshment varied. In an extreme case, a mother who was frequently psychotic and had repeated psychiatric hospitalizations was symbiotically tied to her drug-abusing son. Early in their family therapy, the I.P. left residential treatment. His mother was able to refuse to take him back, but this triggered in her an overt psychotic episode, which was resolved with the help of her psychiatrist. After she emerged from her psychosis, she poignantly told her son, "I will not hold you to me anymore." Enmeshed mothers tend to think, act, and feel for their drug-abusing child. Several mothers in my study regularly took prescription tranquilizers or narcotics, which were shared overtly or covertly with their sons. Many mothers suffered an agitated depression whenever their child "acted out" in destructive ways. Mothers who took prescription tranquilizers or abused alcohol frequently increased their intake whenever the IP acted out (Kaufman & Kaufmann, 1979). Such mothers will do anything for their addict sons except leave them alone (Fort, 1954). In a study of mothers of drug addicts, schizophrenics, and controls, the need for the child was greatest in the mothers of drug abusers (Attardo, 1965). Many mothers experienced alcohol abuse, suicide attempts, and severe psychosomatic symptoms, which were blamed on the addict, thereby reinforcing the pattern of guilt and mutual manipulation.

The relationship between mothers and drug-abusing daughters will be discussed in Chapter 4. One father committed suicide after his wife ordered him out of the house for his brutality. A third of fathers were alcoholic, but all but four of these had abandoned their families or died from alcoholism and had not been a part of treatment.

Most studies of the fathers of drug abusers find the incidence of parental alcoholism to be about 50 percent (Ziegler-Driscoll, 1979). Ziegler-Driscoll also noted a very high incidence of alcoholism and single parents in the families of Black addicts. The one father in my study who had himself been a heroin addict had four other children beside the index patient who were heroin addicts.

In totally enmeshed families, both parents frequently collaborate to keep the addict infantilized under the guise of protection from arrest or other dangers. The pattern of father–son brutality was quite common in my study, although it was seen both in fathers who were enmeshed and disengaged. With disengaged fathers, brutality was frequently their only contact with their children. However, enmeshed fathers also beat their children, which pushed the IP into a coalition with the mother against the father. Physical brutality was common between Italian fathers and their sons. However, this was a multigenerational problem, which was a part of enmeshed intimacy. It is much easier for these fathers to hit a child once or twice than to enforce discipline over hours or days. In one Mexican-American family in my study, the father was described by his son as disengaged. However, he attended every family session, and after a while his "machismo" lessened so that he was able to tell his son that he frequently worried about him so much that it impaired his functioning at work.

Overt incest was reported only in one father–daughter pair in my sample, but it was suspected or experienced covertly in many other parent–child and sibling pairs. This is a much lower incidence of incest than has been reported in many recent studies of female addicts and may be a function of the predominant use of a group setting or the therapists' lack of emphasis on this issue. Kaufman and Kaufmann's (1979) studies at Phoenix House showed an 80-percent incidence of incest in female addicts.

Most of the fathers who in my study were very hard workers set very high performance standards for their sons; the standards were not met or even approached. Many sons worked directly for their fathers, and thus were frequently protected from having to meet the usual demands of employment. Several fathers suffered disabling physical injuries after the onset of their son's drug dependence, which prevented them from continuing to work.

Although addicts frequently appear to be uninvolved with their parents, a closer examination of their contacts reveals that they are quite involved despite their many futile attempts at individuation.

Other Relevant Studies

In a study of addicts, Stanton (1977) noted that 82 percent of addicts with living parents saw their mothers and 58 percent saw their fathers at least weekly; 66 percent either lived with their parents or saw their mothers daily. In 1966, Vaillant reported that 72 percent of addicts still lived with their mothers at age 22, and 47 percent continued to live with a female blood relative after age 30. Vaillant also noted that virtually all of the 30 abstinent addicts in his follow-up study were living apart from their parents. Stanton and Todd's (1982) review of the literature strongly supports the greater involvement of addicts than non-addicts with their families. They found that 15 of 17 reports on living arrangements and all seven on frequency of family contact supported the pattern of addict overinvolvement with their families.

Other studies of addict families are worthy of discussion, although many are characterized by limited socioeconomic sampling and lack of quantification. Fort (1954) noted the "frequent virtual absence of a father figure" in a group comprised mainly of ghetto addicts. Studies of middle-class families have noted the presence of a "strong" father (Alexander & Dibb, 1975). Kirschenbaum, Leonoff, and Maliano (1974) noted that "the father's position as strong leader of the family seemed to be a fiction . . . needed and nourished by the mother as the 'real head of the family'." Schwartzman (1975) also noted that fathers were either "strawman" authoritarian figures or distant, but clearly "secondary" to the mother in terms of power.

Noone and Reddig (1976) noted that drug use is essential to maintaining an interactional family equilibrium that resolves a disorganization of the family system which existed prior to drug taking. The "addictor" or person who leads to addiction in the system may be the parent(s) or the spouse, according to Pearson and Little (1975). Wellisch, Gay, and McEntea (1970) noted that one partner, usually the male, is supported or taken care of by the other and so becomes an "easy rider" throughout the relationship. My experience has been that the male addict dominates either the addicted or non-addicted spouse to take care of him in much the same way he related to the mother. This pattern was particularly clear in Puerto Rican addicts.

Stanton and Todd's (1982) extensive work with addicts' families involved a large data base including over 450 videotapes of interactional sessions. They felt that the patterns they observed differed more in degree than in kind from the observations of others. When a male addict begins to succeed in any way that leads him toward leaving the family, a crisis occurs in the family that draws him back so that he reverts to "failure behavior." Families of addicts differ from other problematic families in: a high frequently of multigenerational chemical dependance, more primitive and direct expressions of conflict, strong explicit family ties, a preponderance of death themes and early separations, and parent–child cultural disparity. The pseudoindividuation in these families permits the addicts to simultaneously be both in and out of his family—both close and distant and competent and incompetent (Stanton et al., 1982).

One basic pattern I have observed is compatible with others' observations of the families of drug abusers, alcoholics, and schizophrenics: a mother and son are symbiotically tied to each other prior to the onset of the symptom, with a father who is excluded and reacts with disengagement and/or brutality. However I have observed factors that have not been sufficiently developed in the literature:

1. *The family patterns of narcotic addicts vary in different ethnic groups.* The father may be disengaged in white Protestant and black families but enmeshed in Italian and Jewish families. Larger samples of families from each ethnic group must be studied with more rigorous methods to clearly delineate these patterns. The communication patterns of families with a heroin

addict are quite different from those of schizophrenics. Double binds are much clearer and less confusing, but frequently the only escape route available to the adolescent is through drugs.

2. *Siblings are of crucial importance,* through their own addiction, which is enmeshed with that of the identified patient, their role as a parental, authoritarian child, or as an extreme success with which the potential addict cannot compete. Addicts may themselves have been parental children who have no way of asking for relief but through drugs. More commonly, they are the youngest child and their addiction maintains them as the baby.

3. *Addict spouse pairs frequently duplicate with each other roles that they have developed in their families of origin* and that may not be correctible unless work is done with the original family as well as the nuclear family.

————————————————————————————— REFERENCES

Alexander, B.K., & Dibb, G.S. Opiate addicts and their parents. *Family Process*, 1975, *14*, 499–514.

Attardo, N. Psychodynamic factors in the mother–child relationship in adolescent drug addiction: A comparison of mothers of schizophrenics and mothers of normal adolescent sons. *Psychotherapeutic Psychosomatic*, 1965, *13*, 249–255.

Cleveland, M. Families and adolescent drug abuse: Structural analysis of children's roles. *Family Process*, 1981, *20*, 295–304.

Fort, J.P. Heroin addiction among young men. *Psychiatry*, 1954, *17*, 251.

Hendin, H., Pollinger, A., Ulman, R., & Carr, A.C. Adolescent marijuana abusers and their families. National Institute on Drug Addiction research monograph 40, Department of Health, Education and Welfare, Wash., D.C. 1981.

Kaufman, E. Family Structures of Narcotic Addicts, *International Journal of the Addictions* 1981, 16:2, 273–282.

Kaufman, E., & Kaufmann, P. From a psychodynamic to a structural understanding of drug dependency. In E. Kaufman & P. Kaufmann (Eds.): *The family therapy of drug and alcohol abuse*. New York: Gardner Press, 1979.

Kirschenbaum, M., Leonoff, G., & Maliano, A. Characteristic patterns in drug abuse families. *Family Therapy*, 1974, *1*, 43–62.

Noone, R.J., & Reddig, R.L. Case studies on the family treatment of drug abuse. *Family Process*, 1976, *15*, 3.

Pearson, M.M., & Little, R.B. Treatment of drug addiction: Private practice experience with 84 addicts. *American Journal of Psychiatry*, 1975, *122*, 164–169.

Reilly, D.M. Family factors in the etiology and treatment of youthful drug abuse. *Family Therapy*, 1976, *2*, 149.

Schwartzman, J. The addict abstenance and the family. *American Journal of Psychiatry*, 1975, *132*, 154–147.

Stanton, M.D. Some outcome results and aspects of structural family therapy with drug addicts. *The Proceedings of the National Drug Abuse Conference*, San Francisco. Cambridge, Mass.: Hall-Schenkman, 1977, May 5–9.

Stanton, M.D., & Todd, T.C. *The family therapy of drug abuse and addiction*. New York: Guilford Press, 1982.

Wellisch, D.K., Gay, G.R., & McEntea, R. The easy rider syndrome: A pattern of hetero- and homosexual relationships in a heroin addict population. *Family Process*, 1970, *9*(3), 425–430.

Valliant, G. A 12-year follow-up of New York narcotic addicts. *Archives of General Psychiatry*, 1966, *15*, 599–609.

Ziegler-Driscoll, G. The similarities in families of drug dependents and alcoholics. In E. Kaufman & P. Kaufmann (Eds.), *Family therapy of drug and alcohol abuse*. New York: Gardner Press, 1979.

Chapter 4

Female Substance Abusers: Psychopathology, Personality, and Family Systems

Until recently, alcoholics have been written about as if they were all males, with relatively little attention paid to the personality, psychopathology, and family aspects of the female. In this chapter, drug and alcohol abuse are combined because many of the problems of women that are associated with drug or alcohol abuse are similar and related to their minority status. If time and knowledge permitted, parallel chapters could also be written on the black, Hispanic, Jewish, Italian, geriatric, etc., substance abuser, but women are certainly our largest minority group.*

On the other hand, there are also vast differences between individual women that must be recognized. Such issues as age, social class, ethnicity, living environment, stage of substance abuse consumption, and historical context (e.g., wars, women's liberation) are extremely important to female substance abusers.

---

*For an excellent review of the effects of ethnic influences on family systems and needs for variations in family treatment, see McGoldrick, Giordano, and Pearce's 1982 book, *Ethnicity in family therapy.*

COMMON ETIOLOGIC FACTORS IN
FEMALE SUBSTANCE ABUSE

Over the past few years many studies of female substance abusers have been published. This work will be summarized, along with my own research and clinical impressions over more than 20 years of working with women substance abusers.

One area of female substance abuse that has received a great deal of attention is the consumption of prescription drugs, which are frequently taken with alcohol and unfortunately are prescribed by male physicians.

Substance abuse by women is very much related to general problems of women in our society, such as lack of social power and external pressures to suppress aspects of themselves that do not conform to female sex-role stereotypes (Sandmaier, 1980). There is still a greater stigma in our society about drinking by women, so they often react with shame and hide their drinking (Corrigan, 1980). Glatt (1979) noted that even women who have lost control of their drinking manage to limit their intake to one or two drinks when dining with their husband or friends. It is not uncommon for women who remain home during the day to drink when alone and nap in the late afternoon, hoping they will appear refreshed when their children and husband return home. Sandmaier (1980) suggests that social denial of women's drinking continues because its feared consequences, such as sexuality and family neglect, violate traditional female stereotypes. The female's ability to hide her drinking may account for much of the telescoping (shorter duration between onset of drinking and alcoholism) described in female alcoholics (Beckman, 1975). Women who work are able to hide substance abuse through nonchallenging jobs and extensive absenteeism (Reichman, 1983). Female alcoholics may readily lose their spousal functions but desperately and tenuously cling to their role as mother (Corrigan, 1980), which may also minimize the attention paid to their drinking. Most women alcoholics described that their husbands drank with them yet disapproved of their drinking (Corrigan, 1980). Fifty-seven percent of women alcoholics reported difficulties in their role as wife, 42 percent as mother. Forty-four percent were unable to carry out their role as wife, 36 percent as mother (Corrigan, 1980). Thus, not unexpectedly—based on social mores—women hold onto their role as mother more dearly than their role as wife. Beckman also suggested that drinking by women may be caused more by pressure, particularly loss, than is male drinking. However, women may often use pressures to *justify* alcoholic drinking, and attributing heavy drinking to a specific traumatic incident is to be avoided (Gomberg, 1980).

Women cannot escape the message many of them have been given throughout their lives: that they are less worthy because they are women. The culturally defined behaviors demanded of women not only do not protect them against alcohol problems but may actually *cause* much of the pain and conflict that lead them to drink. Studies consistently show that women drink to relieve loneliness, feelings of inferiority, and conflicts about their sex role, regardless of their lifestyle (Sandmaier, 1980).

PSYCHOPATHOLOGY IN FEMALE SUBSTANCE ABUSERS

Women select their drugs for a variety of reasons, but there is no clear evidence for hypotheses that relate specific drug choices in women to specific dynamic conflicts or personality. However, women tend to use drugs more to cope with life, whereas men state they use them more for social reasons or pleasure. Women are not only as vulnerable to drug use by female peers as are men, but they also are more susceptible to receiving drugs from boyfriends and spouses. Hendin 1980 has attempted to find specific dynamics for specific drugs and speculates that women may use stimulant drugs like amphetamines to push themselves in directions that they think they should pursue but which are blocked by inner feelings.

Most early clinical reports supported the concept that psychopathology was more frequent in women substance abusers than in males. This concept is in keeping with my earlier stated hypothesis that the more deviant a behavior is from selected norms, the more likely it is to be associated with psychopathology (Kaufman, 1976). Thus, we would expect female alcoholics and hard drug abusers (i.e., heroin, PCP, cocaine), but not female abusers of prescription drugs, to be sicker than their male counterparts. We also would expect polydrug abusers to be sicker than those who prefer a single drug or class of drugs, regardless of sex. However, it is difficult to separate pre-existing pathology from the social consequences of substance abuse, which are more severe in women. One consistent finding is a higher incidence of depression in female alcoholics than in males. Winokur and Pitts (1965) were among the early authors who related alcoholism in women to affective illness. Schuckit (1969) found that 27 percent (19) of 70 female alcoholics had suffered severe depression prior to their alcoholism. Winokur, Reich, Rimmer, and Pitts (1970) described a "depressive spectrum disease" in which women with severe depression have a high incidence of first-degree male relatives with sociopathy or alcoholism and female relatives with a high incidence of depression. Winokur and Clayton (1968) speculated, based on genetic studies of depression and alcoholism, that alcoholism may be a different illness in women than men. This may only be true for that minority of alcoholic women who have a strong affective component to their illness. It has also been noted that female alcoholics have a higher incidence of suicide attempts than males, although this may be related to higher suicide attempt rates in women in general (Winokur & Clayton, 1968).

Utilization of the Brief Psychiatric Rating Scale has demonstrated that female chronic alcoholics score higher than males in anxiety, guilt, tension, depressed mood, hostility, and neuroticism (Hoffman & Wefring (1972). Bromet and Moos (1976) felt these to be consistent findings and postulated that they may be related to the fact that more male than female alcoholics are married and to the overall greater mental health of married alcoholics of both sexes.

Studies of male and female heroin addicts, however, only partially support the hypothesis that female addicts demonstrate greater psychopathology. In a review of 15 studies of psychopathology in female drug abusers, 5 (33 percent) found that females functioned more poorly than males, and no studies supported the opposite conclusion. Four studies made no comparisons to males. Six studies (40 percent) did not report broad male/female differences, instead noting psychological difficulties in both male and female drug abusers (Burt, Glynn, & Sowder, 1979). DeLeon (1974) has found greater evidence of anxiety and depression in female addicts, and DeLeon and Jain-chill (1980) found more emotional disturbance and psychosomatic symptoms in women addict clients. Ellinwood, Smith, and Vaillant (1966) diagnosed women addicts as more often neurotic (10 percent) and psychotic 7 percent (males 1 percent, 0 percent) and males as more often suffering from personality disorders (77 percent) and sociopathic (17 percent) (females 66 percent, 3 percent).

Based on these studies, it is my conclusion that female substance abusers have a greater degree of psychopathology than males. However, as substance use by females becomes more condoned by society, we are seeing an equalization of psychopathology between male and female abusers.

PERSONALITY ASPECTS OF FEMALE SUBSTANCE ABUSERS

Minnesota Multiphasic Personality Inventory (MMPI) studies of female addicts parallel the above studies of psychopathology. According to Hill, Haertzen, and Davis (1962), the typical female addict has a "neurotic psychopath" profile with high elevations on depression and paranoid scales, whereas the typical male addict shows an "indifferentiated psychopath" profile. Women alcoholics have been found to have higher scores on the MMPI Neurotic triad: neurasthenia, hysteria, and depression (Zelen et al., 1966). However, the mean profiles of male and female alcoholics resemble each other more in personality characteristics than do those of non-alcoholic men and women (Beckman, 1975). Both male and female alcoholics had high scores of depression, psychasthenia, and psychopathy (Zelen et al., 1966). Rosen (1960) found the women's overall profiles were different from men's but that women alcoholics and matched women psychiatric outpatients showed marked similarities in MMPI profiles.

According to Blane (1968), an essential feature of alcoholism in women is a preoccupation with being inadequate and inept and futility about finding a way to establish themselves in their social environment. Compared to non-alcoholic women, female alcoholics see themselves as less socially competent and less effective in goal achievement. They have more covert and overt anxiety, and feel unworthy and dissatisfied with their purpose in life (McLachlan, Walderman, Birchmore & Marsden, 1979). Thus, women start heavier drinking later than men, when they realize that they cannot fulfil the promises of their youth (Blane, 1968). About 20 percent of women start misusing alcohol during a middle-age identity crisis precipitated by a situational event (Beckman, 1975). In a related study of college students, the lower the expectation of satisfaction of needs, the greater the recourse to alcohol, especially among women (Jessor, Carman, & Grossman, 1968).

Most clinicians agree that women's alcoholism is more "telescoped" than men's: i.e., that their alcoholism begins after much shorter periods of problem drinking. Related to this phenomenon is another common generalization: that women are more likely than men to begin problem drinking in response to a specific traumatic event, even with no prior history of alcohol abuse. Most of these traumas involve losses that are threats to their sense of personal adequacy, including divorce, desertion, infidelity, death of a family member, a child or last child leaving home (the "empty nest syndrome"), and health problems particularly gynecological and menopausal (Sandmaier, 1980).

The personalities of women substance abusers can be understood most accurately when we look at their various subtypes. Mogar, Wilson & Helm (1970) have described five personality subtypes in women: normal-manic, normal-depressive, hysterical, psychopathic, and passive-aggressive. Hart and Stueland (1980) classified female alcoholics into six personality types (1) passive-impulsive neurotic style, (2) introverted obsessive–compulsive, (3) paranoid, (4) schizoid, (5) trait disorder with psychopathology, and (6) extroverted obsessive–compulsive. The two most common were the normal-manic and normal-depressive, which are marked by hyperfeminity, strong masculine strivings, masochistic tendencies, and confusion over sex roles (Beckman, 1975). Wilsnack (1982) has noted that middle-class women drink as a result of two types of sex role conflicts. In one form, the women's sex role behaviors are inconsistent with her own values. In the other, the woman is not herself conflicted, but her values and activities are in conflict with a social environment which demands sex-stereotyped behavior. Because of this conflict or because of a number of stresses, Wilsnack reported that married women employed outside the home have higher rates of heavy and problem drinking than either unmarried employed women or married unemployed women . However, Sandmeier (1980) found an opposite pattern of sex role conflict among lower-class alcoholic women, who consciously reject the norms of femininity. Alcohol gives them time out from their sex role conflicts; the more they drink the more competent they feel. Another type of assertive female alcoholic who is in the minority (in studies to date) rejects all pressures to be ladylike and good and is generally rebellious. She is broadly defiant, and has problems at school, illegal activities, serious conflicts with parents, sexual permissiveness, abusive drinking, and drug abuse while a teenager (Sandmaier, 1980).

Women heroin addicts may also be divided into two similar types (Rosenbaum, 1981). Women presently over the age of 25 appear to be passive and are introduced to and maintained on heroin by their male mate. Younger women tend to be more liberated and assertive and, in the lower classes, use hard drugs as part of a culture which is powerful, respected, and prestigous. In my own studies of women heroin addicts, most of whom were over 25 and involved with addict mates, the majority were quite passive and their addiction was fused to that of their mates (Kaufman, 1981). However, an impressive minority remained remarkably assertive, most of whom were capable of maintaining their own heroin supplies and, when they completed treatment, were able to achieve a good deal of traditional success. One became a physician, another went through college and became a clinical social worker, and several became excellent program directors and counselors.

Thus we see that although overt passivity and depression are more common in women substance abusers than in men, a growing number of women are quite assertive as well as sociopathic. In addition we see a wide variety of psychopathology, personality styles, and personality disorders in female substance abusers, and these disorders are probably of greater frequency and intensity than in similar males.

FAMILY SYSTEMS OF FEMALE SUBSTANCE
ABUSERS

The Family of Origin

One remarkably consistent finding is the high prevalence
of substance abusers in the families of female substance abusers. Winokur and Clayton's (1968) study of the families of 69
male and 45 female alcoholics revealed that the women had a
higher prevalence of alcoholism in their fathers (28 percent),
mothers (12 percent), and female siblings (12 percent) than did
male alcoholics (21, 3, and 2 percent respectively). Beckman
(1975), in her literature review, noted that, despite one unusually
low estimate of 6 percent, 28 percent was in the low range for
prevalence of alcoholism in the fathers of women alcoholics and
that estimates as high as 50 percent were common. There is
evidence that in the future progressively more female alcoholics
will be the daughters of alcoholic mothers. Corrigan (1980)
found that only 3 percent of women alcoholics over age 50 had
ever observed their mother drunk, whereas 55 percent of those
under 30 had. Bromet and Moos (1976) noted that female alcoholics more often have mothers who drink heavily than do male
alcoholics. Binion (1979) found that "drinking a lot" was a more
common problem in the families of heroin addicted women
(59.7 percent) than in matched controls (42.9 percent). Parental
condoning of the use of alcohol and drugs appears to lead to
abuse, even when the parents do not abuse substances themselves (Kandel, 1975).

A very common finding in families of female substance abusers is an emotionally brutal childhood and a high incidence of
familial disruption. Sandmaier (1980) has found that alcoholic
women are more likely than men to have lost one parent through
divorce, desertion, or death during their childhood. Wilsnack
(1982) also noted that alcoholic women have a high rate of family
disruption, including loss of one or both parents through death,
divorce, or separation and alcoholism or psychosis in parents
or close relatives. Gomberg (1980) found that although the rates
of such disruption are high in both alcoholic men and women,
they are higher still in women. Women who have experienced

broken homes before the age of 10 are significantly more likely than men with the same history to become heavy drinkers (Boothroyd, 1980). Many narcotic addicts have experienced early separation or death of a parent, mainly the father (Stanton, 1979). Johnston (1968) found that 65 percent of female narcotics users had parents who separated during their childhood.

Many women alcoholics perceive that they had cold, severe, bossy, domineering mothers and warmer, gentler, but alcoholic fathers (Beckman, 1975). These fathers only rebeled against their dominant wives when drunk. These daughters tended to reject their mothers. They felt that the alcoholic father preferred them to the mother and that if the mother had been more loving, the father would not drink. They gravitated to their fathers for the affection and support they felt they did not receive from their mothers. They also identified with their alcoholic fathers, leaving them directly vulnerable to develop alcoholism as adults. Their lack of a positive female role model left them with a lack of female identity, leading to conflicts that made them indirectly vulnerable to alcoholism. Although the pattern of a weak father who is overinvolved with his daughter is common, the totally absent father is also rather prevalent. So is the pattern of parental mental illness, particularly unipolar depression. The fathers of female alcoholics are more likely to be depressed, mentally ill, or absent than their mothers (Winokur & Clayton, 1968).

In comparison to their non-alcoholic sisters, women alcoholics feel they had more unhappy childhoods with less acceptance and approval (Corrigan, 1980). In an early study, Wall (1937) found that hospitalized female alcoholics had no particularly strong ties to either parent or to sibs, compared to 37 percent of male alcoholics who had a strong attachment to their mothers.

Nurco, Wegner, and Stephenson (1982) have noted that female addicts are more likely to feel guilty about violating their families' expectations than males. As a result of greater dependancy needs, women are also more likely to be involved with their families than males, as well as to become dependent on treatment situations.

The Nuclear Family

A key issue in the families of women substance abusers is substance abuse by the spouse. If both spouses misuse drugs or alcohol, they tend to form a mutually supportive network which accelerates abuse and dependence. Despite this overt support, these relationships are rarely intrinsically loving and eventually deteriorate. Glatt (1979) suggested that the female alcoholic is much more likely to be left by her spouse than when the sexes are reversed. In addition, female alcoholics who are daughters of alcoholic fathers are much more likely to be married to alcoholics (Woodside, 1982). Mutual substance abuse provides a critical focus for the entire relationship. The lives of alcoholic couples revolve around drinking. Heroin-addicted couples do everything together, including "hustling, scoring, fixing, sleeping, and eating" (Rosenbaum, 1981). Although sexuality may be enhanced in the early phases of such relationships, it generally progressively dissipates.

Corrigan (1980) studied the stability of the marriages of 150 alcoholic women. Seventy-two percent (108) had been legally married, but at the time of this interview only 31 percent were married, 30 percent were divorced or separated, 11 percent were widowed, and 27 percent never married. Of the women who suffered marital disruption, in 52 percent it took place six or more years prior to entering treatment. Of the married sample, 27 percent did not drink heavily during the marriage, 46 percent were in their first marriages in which they drank heavily, and about one-fourth drank heavily during a marriage ended by separation or divorce. Only 7 percent of husbands left their wives because of heavy drinking, in contrast to most studies, which state that men often leave their alcoholic wives. Ninety percent of these women were married to husbands who drank, and 42 percent of these described their husband's drinking as "heavy." Fifty-seven percent of these married women had difficulty in their role as wife, and 42 percent had difficulty in their roles as mother; 44 percent and 32 percent respectively stated they were unable to fulfill these roles at all.

The husband of a female alcoholic may initially deny her drinking, perhaps because she hides it so well. He may also be quite critical and rejecting of her drinking, and he may later abandon her. If not, he may become a "co-alcoholic" whose own life is preoccupied with his spouse and her drinking. Generally, men are much less nurturing than women and less willing to nurse along an alcoholic spouse. Men who continue to live with alcoholic spouses may be sociopathic and alcoholic themselves or may have a need to dominate. Another pattern (Glatt, 1979) describes a rigid obsessional man dominated by his wife and enthralled with her acting-out, which is in contrast to his own constricted behavior. Husbands who continue to live with alcoholic wives may have extremely high levels of denial, so that they may experience less frustration (Estes & Baker, 1977).

Alcoholic women have sexual problems but not the general "promiscuity" that was reported in the early literature. An unpublished survey of sexuality in 35 alcoholic women who experienced 3 to 12 months of sobriety in comparison to 35 non-alcoholic controls revealing the following (Covington, 1983): a higher frequency of sexual activity with self (masturbation) but less with partner; less orgasmic response; less satisfaction with sexual relationships; more sexual dysfunction; and more sexual abuse. Forrest (1982) estimated that 20 percent of alcoholic women who enter outpatient psychotherapy for alcoholism are psychosexually dysfunctional and 70 to 80 percent of this group have secondary orgastic dysfunction. Forrest suggested that many sexually dysfunctional alcoholic women drink in order to feel "feminine, sexually aroused, and stimulated," as intoxication permits denial of inability to have an orgasm. Some women who abuse alcohol and drugs frequently begin use to avoid anxieties about sexuality and sexual performance, and continue abuse to relieve ongoing anxieties about sexual dysfunction, finding themselves totally unable to perform sexually in the later stages of alcoholism.

Women heroin addicts tend to be living with an addicted partner. Ninety-three percent of white women and 85 percent of black women entering drug abuse treatment in Michigan, were living with men who abused drugs, compared to 75 percent of white men and 66 percent of black men (Ryan & Moise, 1981). In my experience women become addicted to heroin by their men in a way which reinforces their dependence. A female addict may be prostituted by her male mates to obtain drugs for the pair, and she in turn may depend on him for her supply of drugs or even for injection of her heroin. If she obtains drugs elsewhere the male may beat her, equating her obtaining drugs from someone else with sexual infidelity.

Rosenbaum (1981) described three common motives for a woman living with an addict to use heroin herself: (1) participating in the dealing process, (2) joining the "mood" and the lifestyle, and (3) getting her fair share of the heroin. When a man is dealing heroin, the woman is also likely to be involved in preparing and selling the drug, which is quite available and abundant. A woman who is involved with an addict but not with his lifestyle would feel very lonely and isolated. Many married addicts fight constantly over getting their appropriate share of the heroin, with the male consistently taking the larger share. In times of stress, such as when supplies are low, the partners lie to and steal from one another, thereby undermining trust and mutality. Rosenbaum (1981) offered a convincing reason why men would not want their wives to get addicted: the additional financial burden on the family. However, in my experience, each spouse will be pulled back into addiction after individual attempts to stop using.

Although mothering is the last aspect of social functioning to be lost by female substance abusers, it is generally considered that severe substance abusers are totally inadequate as mothers. Younger drug addicts have more younger children living with them than do older alcoholics (Beschner & Thompson, 1981). Seventy-three percent of female addicts admitted to a Washington, DC treatment program were mothers, and 48 percent of their children were under age 6 (Eldred & Washington, 1976). Rosenbaum (1981) has observed that the heroin-addicted mother who can also take care of her children is respected in the addict world. The better able a mother is to establish an early routine for obtaining her heroin, particularly one where she is involved in successful dealing, the better she is able to devote time to her children (Rosenbaum, 1981). However, even in this type of situation potent or excessive heroin or other sedative use can interfere with mothering ability, as drowsiness leaves her incapable of responding to her child's needs.

When substance-abusing women abandon their children, they frequently turn them over to their own mothers. This is a type of female pseudoindividuation: although the addicted women assumes the adult role of mothering a child, she then returns the child to her own mother, abnegating her adult role and reinforcing her own closeness and dependence on her mother. The grandchild becomes a "gift" for the substance abuser's mother and provides an opportunity for her to frequently visit home and meet her own needs.

Whereas some alcoholic fathers abuse their children sexually and violently, alcoholic mothers are prone to neglect their children. Thus, children of alcoholic parents tend to be fearful, cold, distrustful, rigid and/or reserved, as well as submissive and dependent like their mothers—characteristics typical of children whose parents are angry, distrustful, dependent, and alienated (DHEW, 1978).

In Corrigan's (1981) previously mentioned study, 56 percent of the women denied drinking during pregnancy, 27 percent did not alter their drinking, 7 percent drank more, and 3 percent drank less. Three of the 16 women who drank heavily during pregnancy had children with birth defects (19 percent) as compared with 11 percent of those who claimed they did not drink heavily. The fetal alcohol syndrome will not be described in detail in this book but its effects are very powerful; the syndrome is diagnosed by growth retardation, central nervous system involvement (developmental delay, intellectual impairment) and facial disfigurement (Rosett & Weiner, 1981). In Corrigan's group, the birth defects included congenital heart defects, cleft palate, blindness, and a kidney problem. Thus, in addition to their other difficulties, these children suffer from the emotional problems of the handicapped. The mother who drank during pregnancy may feel very guilty and responsible for her child's defects. She may also react quite negatively to caring for a sick or handicapped child. The child's neurologically-based nonresponsiveness or irritability may cause the mother to withdraw nurturing, leading to further difficulties for the child.

In the absence of fetal alcoholism, there are still problems for the children of alcoholic women. A third of Corrigan's (1980) sample had at least one child with learning difficulties and were contacted for school problems. Over half had reported difficulties with school attendance, but no more frequently than their non-alcoholic sister's children. Eighty percent of these alcoholic women raised their own children. However, 39 percent had been separated from their children for prolonged periods. Fifty-six percent of the women admitted that their mothering was negatively affected by their drinking, and 42 percent stated they had difficulty in caring for their children. Thirty percent of women believed their children were unaffected by their drinking. Husbands tended to agree with their wives on the deleterious effects of their drinking on children, disagreeing with wives who said their children were unaffected (Corrigan, 1980). Estes and Baker (1977) found that all 10 husbands of alcoholic wives in their study felt their children faced emotional and/or physical neglect. These mothers might shower children with attention when sober and abandon them when drunk. They even drove drunk with children in the car.

Some of the differences between the effects of maternal drug abuse and alcohol abuse on children may be class-related, such as the involvement of others in the care of the children of heroin addicts. Mothers who abuse prescription drugs are most probably quite similar to alcoholic mothers if they share ethnicity and social class. There are fetal abnormalities in the children of mothers who use drugs in the first trimester of pregnancy, but these have not been as well documented as in fetal alcohol syndrome (Finnigan & Fehr, 1980). However, if the newborn is addicted at birth (which may occur when the mother is a heroin addict), the withdrawal symptoms may cause the mother to reject a difficult child and start a cycle of maternal rejection and further infant withdrawal, which deprives the infant of much-needed nurturing.

REFERENCES

Beckman, J.J. Women alcoholics: A review of social and psychological studies. *Journal of Studies on Alcohol*, 1975, *36*(7), 797–824.

Beschner, G., & Thompson, P. Women and drug abuse treatment: Needs and services. Washington, D.C.: National Institute on Drug Abuse, Alcohol Drug Abuse Mental Health Administration, 1981.

Binion, V.J. A descriptive comparison of the families of origin of women heroin users and abusers. In *Addicted women: Family dynamics, self-perceptions and support systems*. Washington, D.C.: NIDA

Monograph, Department of Health, Education and Welfare, 1979, 77–113.

Blane, H.T. The personality of the alcoholic: Guises of dependency. New York: Harper & Row, 1968.

Boothroyd, W.E. Nature and development of alcoholism in women. In O.J. Kalaut (Ed.), *Alcohol and drug problems in women.* New York: Plenum Press, 299–329, 1980.

Bromet, E., & Moos, R. Sex and marital status in relation to the characteristics of alcoholics. *Journal of Studies on Alcohol,* 1976, *37*, 1302–1312.

Burt, M.R., Glynn, T.J., & Sowder, B.J. Psychosocial characteristics of drug-abusing women. Rockville, Md.: ADAMHA, Department of Health, Education and Welfare, 1979.

Corrigan, E.M. *Alcoholic women in treatment.* New York/Oxford: Oxford University Press, 1980.

Covington, S. Personal communication, 1983.

DeLeon, G. Phoenix house: Psychopathology among male and female drug-free residents. *Addictive Diseases* 1974, 1(2), 135–152.

DeLeon, G., & Jainchill, N. Female drug abusers: Social and psychological status two years after treatment in a therapeutic community. Presented at the National Alcohol and Drug Conference, Washington, D.C., 1980.

Department of Health, Education and Welfare. Third Special Report to the U.S. Congress on Alcohol and Health, June 1978.

Ellinwood, E.H., Smith, W.G., & Vaillant, G.E. Narcotic addiction in males and females: A comparison. *International Journal of the Addictions,* 1966, *1*, 33–35.

Estes, N.J., & Baker, J.M. Spouses of alcoholic women. In N.J. Estes & M.E. Heinemann (Eds.), *Alcoholism: Development, consequences, and intervention.* St. Louis: C.V. Mosby, 186–193, 1977.

Finnegan, L.F., & Fehr, K.O. The effects of drugs on fetus and newborn. In O.J. Kalant (Ed.), *Alcohol and drug problems in women.* New York: Plenum Press, 653–723, 1980.

Forrest, G.C. *Alcoholism and human sexuality,* Springfield, Ill.: C.C. Thomas, 1982.

Glatt, M.M. Reflections on the treatment of alcoholism in women. *British Journal on Alcohol and Alcoholism,* 1979, *14*(2), 77–83.

Gomberg, E.S. Risk factors related to alcohol problems among women: Proneness and vulnerability. In *Alcoholism and alcohol abuse among women.* Washington, D.C.: Department of Health, Education and Welfare, 1980.

Hart, L.S., & Stueland, D.S. Classifying women alcoholics by Cattell's 16PF. *Journal of Studies on Alcohol,* 1980, *41*, 911–921.

Hendin, H. Psychosocial theory of drug abuse: A psychodynamic approach. In D. Letheri, M. Sayers, & M.W. Pearson, (Eds.), *Theories on drug abuse. National Institute of Drug Abuse Research Monograph 30.* Department of Health, Education and Welfare, March 1980, 195–200.

Hill, H.E., Haertzen, C.A., & Davis, H. An MMPI factor analytic study of alcoholics, narcotic addicts and criminals. *Quarterly Journal of Studies on Alcohol,* 1962, *23,* 411–431.

Hoffman, H., & Welfring, L.R. Sex and age differences in psychiatric symptoms in alcoholics. *Psychological Report,* 1972, *30,* 887–889.

Jessor, R., Carman, R.S., & Grossman, P.H. Expectations of need satisfaction and drinking patterns of college students. *Quarterly Journal of Studies on Alcohol,* 1968, *29,* 101–116.

Johnston, C.W. A descriptive study of 100 convicted female narcotic residents. *Corrective Psychiatry,* 1968, *14,* 230–236.

Kandel, D.B. Stages in adolescent involvement in drug abuse. *Science* 1975, 190, 912—914.

Kaufman, E. The abuse of multiple drugs. *American Journal of Drug and Alcohol Abuse,* 1976, *3*(2), 293–301.

Kaufman, E. Family structures of narcotics addicts. *International Journal of the Addictions,* 1981, *16*(1), 106–118.

McGoldrick, M., Pearce, J.K., & Giordano, J. *Ethnicity and family therapy,* New York: Guilford Press, 1982.

McLachlan, J.F.C., Walderman, R.L., Birchmore, D.F., & Marsden, L.R. Self-evaluation, role satisfaction and anxiety in the woman alcoholic. *International Journal of Addictions,* 1979, *14*(6), 609–832.

Mogar, R.E., Wilson, W.M., & Helm, S.T. Personality subtypes of male and female alcoholic patients. *Internatinal Journal of Addictions,* 1970, 5:99–113.

Nurco, D.N., Wegner, N., & Stephenson, P. Female narcotic addicts: Changing profiles. *Journal of Addiction and Health,* 1982, *3*(2), 66–105.

Reichman, W. Affecting Attitudes and Assumptions About Women and Alcohol Problems. *Alcohol Health and Research World,* 1983, 7(3), 6–10.

Rosen, A.C. A comparative study of alcoholics and psychiatric patients with the MMPI. *Quarterly Journal of Studies on Alcohol,* 1960, *21,* 253–266.

Rosenbaum, M. *Women on heroin.* New Brunswick, N.J.: Rutgers University Press, 1981.

Rosett, H.L., & Weiner, L. Effects of alcohol on the fetus. In E.M. Pattison & E. Kaufman (Eds.), *Encyclopedia handbook of alcoholism*, New York: Gardner Press, 1981, 301–310.

Ryan, V.S., & Moise, R. A comparison of women and men entering drug abuse treatment programs. Women's Drug Research Project Report, Ann Arbor, Michigan, University of Michigan, 1979.

Sandmaier, M. *The invisible Alcoholics: Women and alcohol abuse in America*. McGraw-Hill, 1980, New York.

Schuckit, M.A., Pitts, F.N., Reich, T., King, L.J., & Winokur, G. Alcoholism. I: Two types of alcoholism in women. *Archives of General Psychiatry*, 1969, *20*, 301–306.

Stanton, M.D. Drugs and the family. *Marriage and Family Review*, 1979 2(1), 1–10.

Wall, J.H. A study of alcoholism in women. *American Journal of Psychiatry*, 1937, *93*, 943–955.

Wilsnack, S.C. Alcohol abuse and alcoholism in women. In E.M. Pattison, & E. Kaufman (Eds.), *Encyclopedia handbook of alcoholism*. New York: Gardner Press, 718–735, 1982.

Winokur, G., & Clayton, P.J. Family history studies in comparison of male and female alcoholics. *Quarterly Journal of Studies on Alcohol*, 1968, *29*, 885–891.

Winokur, G., & Pitts, F.N. Affective disorder. VI: A family history study of prevalences, sex differences and possible genetic factors. *Journal of Psychiatric Research*, 1965, *3*, 113–123.

Winokur, G., Reich, T., Rimmer, J., & Pitts, F.N. Alcoholism. III: Diagnosis and familial psychiatry illness in 259 alcoholic probands. Archives of General Psychiatry, 1970, *23*, 104–111.

Woodside, M. Children of alcoholics: A report to Hugh L. Carey, Governor, State of New York. Albany: New York State Division of Alcoholism and Alcohol Abuse, July 1982.

Zelen, S.L., Fox, J., Gould, E., & Olson, R.W. Sex-contingent differences between male and female alcoholics. *Journal of Clinical Psychology*, 1966, *22*, 160–165.

Chapter 5

The Role of Alcohol and Drugs in Family Violence

It is generally agreed that alcohol plays a critical role in domestic, particularly spousal, violence. It was once thought that the superego dissolved under the influence of alcohol, thus allowing individuals who are normally well controlled to give vent to their basic aggressive instincts and perhaps physically hurt those toward whom they are most ambivalent—generally their family. Like all overly simplistic explanations, this one leaves much to be desired, and many other factors need to be examined. The role of drugs in family violence has not been explored in nearly the depth that the role of alcohol has, nor has the interaction between drugs and alcohol and violence.

Alcohol and drugs have been consistently correlated with violent behavior including assaults, violent crimes, and murder. In our society the most violence takes place in the bedroom, followed closely by the kitchen. Twenty-five percent of all murders are intrafamilial, and in over half of these the victim is the spouse (Hindman, 1979). These violent behaviors have been observed with alcohol and drugs, but it has not been proven definitely that the substance abuse is causal. I feel that alcohol and drugs play a critical role in domestic violence in a wide variety of ways as these substances interact synergistically with a multitude of other factors. This topic is extremely important to family therapists because violence is such a common characteristic in families with a substance abuser.

75

NEUROPHYSIOLOGIC ASPECTS

Several of the models that explain the effects of alcohol and other drugs on violence are physiologic. Alcohol's effects on the brain are quite similar to the effects of sedatives, hypnotics, and minor tranquilizers. Alcohol tends to have a sedative effect while the blood alcohol level (BAC) is increasing and an agitating effect when the BAC is decreasing (Gitlow, 1981). This biphasic effect is also seen with short-acting sedative drugs. During the sedating phase, which lasts about 2 hours, alcohol may lead to violence by diminishing anxiety about consequences, lowering inhibitions, and/or giving the drinker a feeling of strength and energy. The agitated phase is a period of increased psychomotor activity, experienced even by social drinkers. Phenomena seen in this agitated period include insomnia, agitation, elevated pulse and blood pressure, tremulousness, and an increased sensitivity to seizures. It seems reasonable that individuals in such a state of neuromuscular irritability would have a lowered ability to tolerate frustration, and would be more impulsive and more easily provoked to violence. As additional evidence for psychophysiologic pathways of alcohol and violence, human subjects who ingest alcohol report an increase in aggressive fantasies and feelings of power and dominance (Zeichner & Pihl, 1979). Laboratory studies support the finding of increased aggressive behavior in subjects who consume alcohol and also in subjects who take placebos with the belief that they contain alcohol (Lang, Goeckner, & Adesso, 1975), so it appears that expectations interact with physiology.

Drugs and alcohol certainly impair cognitive functioning and thus impair the individual's perception of a situation: how threatening it is, how dangerous violent behavior would be, and the consequences of violence. Misperceptions and distortions of consequence may lead to taking risks of violence that would not be taken if the person were in a more rational state.

- The sedative drugs are physiologically similar to alcohol. They may initially produce behavioral excitation, stimulation, and lack of inhibition rather than the usual sedation. The "high" is a disinhibition euphoria that depends on personality, setting, and expectation. The user may become happy, pleasant, euphoric, and "mellow" or hostile, suspicious, aggressive, and violent. Barbiturates are frequently implicated in aggravated assault charges. Low-dose effects are erratic, but moderate to high doses slow down reaction time and impair complicated mental functions, inhibition, emotional control, and physical coordination (Wesson & Smith, 1973). The minor tranquilizers react quite similarly: Normal doses usually provide relaxation and well-being, but with excessive doses there may be disorientation, confusion, memory impairment, personality alterations, rage reactions (Patch, 1974), and other symptoms resembling drunkenness. Rage reactions on moderate doses of chlordiazepoxide and diazepam have been reported (Patch, 1974). Neuropsychological impairment has been noted even after 2 months of abstinence from severe polydrug abuse (Judd & Grant, 1975). This type of impairment can also lead to impulsivity and low frustration tolerance, which lead in turn to violence. Withdrawal symptoms from sedatives include anxiety, irritability, confusion, and paranoia, all of which can facilitate the expression of violence in family and other settings.

- Heroin and other narcotics are well known for their rage-reduction effects. However, even these drugs may also act on some individuals as stimulants and activators (Hoffman, 1975) and thereby facilitate violence.

- Amphetamines, particularly in high doses, can cause suspiciousness, hyperactivity, and sudden episodes of assaultive and even homicidal behavior. With large doses, usually docile caged mice will slaughter each other (Kramer & Pinco, 1973). Amphetamine abusers often alternately use sedatives to relax or sleep; this combination may also lead to increased violence.

- Cocaine, with similar stimulating qualities to amphetamines, is not as often reported in association with violence, although it can lead to gross paranoia. The lack of association of cocaine and violence may possibly be due to its expense, and pattern of use which generally mitigates against doses high enough to lead to violence. However, the more potent "freebase" cocaine is associated with higher levels of anxiety and potential for violence (Wilford, 1981).

- The use of LSD and other hallucinogens frequently leads to violence through anxiety, irritability, and misperception of situations as harmful. However, no hallucinogen has been as frequently associated with violence as phenylcyclidine (PCP). In monkeys, rats and mice, PCP produced behavior effects similar to those of amphetamines (Balster & Chait, 1978), with the additional effect of ataxia, although in lower doses it may be sedating. PCP also causes sedation at times in humans, initiating a catatonic state. It may also lead to a hyperactive state including agitation, excitement, hostility, marked negativism, and violent psychotic behavior (Peterson & Stillman, 1978). PCP use is frequently associated with violent, assaultive, combative, suicidal, and homocidal behavior (Siegel, 1978). PCP may also induce hypersexuality, leading to rape and assault. If the PCP user's goal-directed activity is overtly frustrated or if frustrations are inferred by distorted perceptions, panic and extreme aggression can occur.

Only in a small percentage of cases do drugs and alcohol lead to violence of any sort. Why violence associated with drug and alcohol use occurs at some times and not at others leads us to look for other interacting causes of domestic violence.

FAMILY FACTORS

There is no unique pattern of family interaction that is related to substance abuse, but there are characteristic interactions and trends, and very often individuals act out with their families the "script" that society has written for them.

Over 6 million incidents of serious physical abuse occur in American families each year. Although women are the aggressors about half the time now, they are still much more often injured, because they are at a physical disadvantage. Family violence is not limited to any social, economic, age, or racial group. Women frequently do not report violence until it is life-threatening because they feel so trapped (Hindman, 1979). They feel incompetent and worthless and that the beatings are therefore deserved. Besides their helplessness, women stay in these relationships because the violence alternates with periods of love, tenderness, and caring (Hindman, 1979). The violent periods get longer and closer together, but these women stay because they are kept penniless and powerless (Hindman, 1979).

One characteristic of alcohol-related domestic violence is its multigenerational repetitiveness: parental abuse, regardless of accompanying violence, significantly increases the risk that the child will become sociopathic and violent prone (Robins, 1966). Sixty-three percent of abused children had at least one grandparent who was alcoholic or abused alcohol. In forty-one percent of cases where both child and spouse abuse occurred, one or both parents had been abused by an alcoholic parent. In ninety percent of the cases where the parent had been an abused child, alcohol was involved in the abuse. Male alcoholics were frequently abused as children and subsequently used physical discipline in their own children (Sanchez-Dirks, 1979).

The spouse and the children are equally liable to be victims of the alcoholic's violence. Gelles (1972) studied 44 violent families. In 21 families (48 percent) drinking accompanied the violence, which was almost always perpetrated by the male. The wives in this study felt that alcohol caused the violence and that when their husbands were sober they were neither violent nor abusive. Protective–reactive violence, which is generally perpetrated by the female, involves an attack because of fear of being attacked. Heavy objects or knives are often used. There may also be "one-way" violence where the physically weaker party (usually the wife) does not hit back for fear of being struck again even harder.

Many arguments are triggered by drinking and drunkenness. Fights start over how much alcohol has been consumed and whether the spouse is drunk or not, and may escalate over related sensitive matters. The ensuing verbal fights are intense and use ammunition from a wide range of issues in the relationship. Eventually, the only way (short of separation) to halt the mutual verbal abuse is physical.

Alcohol is frequently used as an excuse or a disavowal of responsibility for violence. The alcoholic may maintain that the family is normal, instead blaming alcohol itself for the deviant act. However, alcohol also may serve as a trigger to explode longstanding marital disputes (Gelles, 1972).

Alcohol is one of several measures which are used to deal with problems in the marriage, which go out of control and lead to violence rather than to solutions. Other solutions which may lead in turn to violence include: threatening to leave (but never leaving), slapping a spouse to stop nagging, flirting to "wake up" a spouse, or throwing an object to prove a point.

CHILD ABUSE

Westermeyer and Bearman (1973) stated that child abuse is so closely related to alcoholism that the incidence of child abuse could be used as an indicator of the prevalence of alcoholism in a population. Parents who are heavily under the influence of alcohol and/or drugs are generally incapable of parenting and thus neglect their children. However, Orme and Rimmers' (1981) recent review on this subject concluded that there was little empirical data to support a relationship between alcoholism and child abuse. Nevertheless, the studies they cited listed between 11.9 percent and 65 percent of child abusers as alcoholics. They ruled this out as evidence using the somewhat specious argument that 5 to 50 percent of people are alcoholic, depending on the population studied. Generally there is more evidence of child neglect than of physical abuse in substance-abusing families.

WIFE ABUSE

Alcohol use by the wife is another important factor in understanding family violence. If a man beats his wife when she is drinking he may blame her drunken behavior for his violence. Alcoholic wife-beaters are frequently violent outside of the home as well. Heroin-addicted husbands may attempt to control their wives. If not addicted, a wife is expected to turn over all of the family's available money for heroin and is threatened and occasionally beaten if she doesn't comply. If addicted, she may be expected to prostitute to get money for the pair and may be beaten if she is suspected of withholding money or of buying or injecting her own heroin.

INTERGENERATIONAL ABUSE

A review of the families of individuals whose deaths were PCP-related revealed that in 30 percent of cases the child was reared in a family where there was physical fighting, which often involved the deceased. However, 57 percent of the victims were involved in physical fights outside of the family (Heiling, Diller, & Nelson, 1982). A form of brutality that female substance abusers commonly experienced in childhood is rape and/or incest. An alcohol treatment program director cited by Wilsnack (1981) stated that 85 percent of the women entering his treatment program had experienced incest or sexual abuse. Twenty-eight percent of father–daughter incest nationally is related to paternal alcohol dependence (Julian, Mohr, & Lapp, 1980). A high incidence of incest and sexual abuse during childhood has also been consistently been found in the histories of female heroin addicts (Ziegler-Driscoll, 1982).

TREATMENT IMPLICATIONS

In the treatment of family violence related to substance abuse, it is essential that the substance abuse or dependence be addressed first. Otherwise any apparent success in reducing the violence will be only temporary. Although treating substance abuse does not necessarily stop violence, it is far easier to treat the violence if the substance abuse problem is resolved first (Hindman, 1979).

In addition to the usual modalities for treatment of substance abuse, families may benefit considerably from support groups that deal specifically with the problems of family violence (e.g., Parents United). Since family violence may constitute a psychiatric emergency, families can gainfully participate in these groups at the onset of their treatment, while they are beginning to deal with their substance abuse problem.

Balster, R.L., Chait, L.D. The behavioral effects of phencyclidine in animals; PCP abuse: An appraisal. In P.C. Peterson, & R.C. Stillman (Eds.), *Nida Research Monograph 21.* Rockville, Md: Department of Health, Education and Welfare, 1978, 53–65.

Gelles, R.J. *The violent home.* Beverly Hills, Calif.: Sage Publications, 1972.

Gitlow, S. The clinical pharmacology and drug interactions of ethanol. In E.M. Pattison & E. Kaufman (Eds.), *Encyclopedia Handbook of Alcoholism.* New York: Gardner Press, 1981, 354–366.

Heilig, S.M., Diller, J., & Nelson, F.L. A study of 44 PCP related deaths. *International Journal of the Addictions,* 1982, *17*(7), 1175–1184.

Hindman, M.H. Family violence. *Alcohol Health and Research World,* 1979, 4(1), 2–11.

Hoffman, F.G. *A Handbook on Drug and Alcohol Abuse.* London, England, Oxford University Press, 1975.

Judd, L.L., & Grant, I. Brain dysfunction in chronic sedative users. *Journal of Psychedelic Drugs,* 1975, *7,* 143–150.

Julian, V., Mohr, C., & Lapp, J. Father–daughter incest: A descriptive analysis. In W.M. Holder (Ed.), *Sexual abuse of children: Implications for treatment.* Englewood, Colorado: American Humane Association, 1980.

Kramer, J., & Pinco, R.G. Amphetamine use and misuse: A medicolegal view. In D.E. Smith & D.R. Wesson (Eds.), *Uppers and Downers.* Englewood Cliffs, N.J.: Prentice Hall, 9–22, 1973.

Lang, A.R., Goeckner, P.J., & Adesso, V.J. Effects of alcohol on aggression in male social drinkers. *Journal of Abnormal Psychology,* 1975, *84*(5), 505–518.

Orme, T.C., Rimmer, J. Alcoholism and child abuse. *Journal of Studies on Alcohol,* 1981, *42*(3), 273–287.

Patch, V.D. Dangers of diazepam, a street drug. *New England Journal of Medicine,* 1974, *290*(14), 807.

Peterson, R.C., & Stillman, R.C. Phencyclidine: An overview. In P. Peterson, & R.C. Stillman (Eds.), *PCP Abuse: An appraisal.* NIDA Research Monograph 21, ADAMHA, Washington, D.C., 1–17, 1978.

Robins, L. Deviant children grown up: A sociological and psychiatric study of sociopathic personality. Baltimore: Williams & Wilkins, 1966.

Sanchez-Dirks, R. Reflections on family violence. *Alcohol, Health and Research World,* 1979, 4(1), 12–16.

Siegel, R.K. Phencyclidine and ketamine intoxication: A study of four populations of recreational users. *Petersen and Stillman*, (Eds.), *PCP Abuse: An Appraisal*, NIDA Research Monograph, ADAMHA, Washington, D.C., 119–147, 1978.

Wesson, D.R., Smith, D.E. Barbiturate toxicity and the treatment of barbiturate dependence. *Smith and Wesson*, (Eds.), *U:ppers and Downers* Englewood Cliffs, New Jersey, Prentice Hall, 1973, 85–96, 1973.

Westermeyer, J., Bearman, J. A proposed social indicator system for alcohol related problems. *Preventive Medicine*, 1973, *2*, 438–444.

Wilford, B.B., *Drug Abuse: A guide for the primary care physician*, American Medical Association, Chicago, Ill., 1981.

Wilsnack, S.C. Alcohol abuse and alcoholism in women. In E.M. Pattison & E. Kaufman (Eds.), *Encyclopedic Handbook of Alcoholism*. New York: Gardner Press, 1981.

Zeichner, A., Pihl, R.O. Effect of alcohol and behavior contingencies on human aggression. *Journal of Abnormal Psychology*, 1979, *88*(2), 153–160.

Ziegler-Driscoll, G. Childhood sexual abuse in substance abusing women: A Therapeutic concern. *In Mimeo*, presented at ADPA, Washington, D.C., August, 1982.

Part III

TREATMENT BACKGROUND

Chapter 6

History of Approaches to Treatment of Substance Abusers

HISTORY

An historical overview of treatment approaches to substance abuse is included not only for understanding but because many of these techniques are essential to present methods of treating families and nonfamilies alike.

One of the most effective treatments for drug abuse is the therapeutic community (TC). Although the TC was first developed in the late 1950s by Maxwell Jones (1968), it was not applied to drug abusers until 1958 by Chuck Dederich III. Dederich, who began Synanon, was greatly influenced by his participation in Alcoholics Anonymous (AA). While Dederich had ideas of his own from the very beginning, there was initially a close rapport between AA and Synanon. After approximately 9 months, Synanon moved apart from Alcoholics Anonymous (Leach, Norris, Darcey, & Bissell, 1969). However, all TCs show significant impact of AA on their basic principles and techniques.

The origins of Alcoholics Anonymous are generally agreed to have been in meetings in Akron, Ohio, beginning in 1935, under the leadership of a man known until recently only as Bill W. Part of the impetus for the formation of AA came from a mystical experience Bill W. had while being treated for alcoholism in Towns Hospital in New York City in 1934 (Wilson, 1957). However, the concept of AA began in a 1932 conversation between an alcoholic American patient and his Swiss psychiatrist, Carl Jung.

AA also derived substantially from the Oxford Group Religious Movement. Ebby T., an old boarding-school acquaintance of Bill and an alcoholic who was helped by the Oxford Group Movement, guided Bill before, during, and after his mystical experience. Immediately after his discharge from Towns Hospital, Bill joined the Oxford Group at the Calvary Church Parish House in New York under the direction of Dr. Samuel Shoemaker, an Episcopal clergyman and here began A.A. As did Synanon, AA later went its own way. Many innovations of the Oxford Group, such as attack therapy in encounter-type groups, have been retained through present-day TCs.

Chuck Dederich attempted to construct a program that would appeal to both addicts and alcoholics, but it was not congenial to alcoholics. Within 6 months, most alcoholics had left the program and begun their own meetings. Dederich proved a skillful and effective innovator, and two of his innovations— residential treatment and secularism—are crucial to contemporary TC's.

Synanon was unique for its time in being exclusively residential in nature. Residential treatment has two distinct advantages: it provides an environment generally free of alcohol and drugs, and it provides an intensive therapeutic experience every waking hour. Another difference is also quite significant: Alcoholics Anonymous espouses a God-centered theology, while Synanon espouses a secular ideology. In terms of the increasing secularization of civilized life, this change may eventually do more to involve people in self-help movements than any other single step. Whether secular or sacred, a form common to all of these organizations is an intensely held, highly cherished belief system (Glaser, 1974). Part of this belief is that their form of self-help, be it AA or a TC, is the only way that the serious substance abuser can be helped—that all other treatment is harmful or at the least a waste of time. The recovered substance abuser imparts this message with a religous fervor that can only come from self-salvation. Although this enthusiasm is helpful, if not essential, to the effectiveness of these treatments, the narrowness of the approach may limit the incorporation or addition of many other helpful approaches as well as preventing the implementation of individualized treatment programs.

TREATMENT PRINCIPLES OF THE THERAPEUTIC COMMUNITY

These techniques are generally for treating heroin addicts. When used with alcoholics and polydrug abusers they are less structured and confronting.

The Role Model

As a substance abuser matures through a program, he or she identifies with varying kinds of therapists. In most programs the first therapist the client meets is a recent graduate or advanced member of the program. These therapists are very much like the client in attitude and language, yet they have "made it," that is, they have stopped using drugs even though they have come from an environment similar to the patient's. They may offer a highly emotional rendering of their own struggle to give up drugs, with which the client can identify. They may share difficult experiences in their own life prior to giving up drugs. They demonstrate that they are not where they are through magic. Frequently, the substance abuser is quite "hungry" to identify with a strong accepting figure of the same sex, because prior contracts with such individuals have been so limited (Kaufman, 1973). Identification facilitates confrontation through empathy which permits the therapist to join with the client supportively while the client recognizes and relinquishes undesirable aspects of his or her personality. Identification is also extremely helpful in work with alcoholics, so much so that an AA member or other recovering/recovered alcoholic can be a useful and often necessary adjunct in the therapy of alcoholics and their families.

Love and Concern

An atmosphere of love and concern must pervade the treatment program at all times. This attitude, together with identification, permit defenses to be stripped. Love and concern are
given in return for adult and giving behavior, painful insights,
and emotional catharsis. At times love and concern are expressed
by reassuring physical gestures such as hand-holding or
embracing. The therapist sets the tone for this kind of interaction, but most of it goes on among members (Kaufman &
DeLeon, 1978).

Confrontation and Encounter

In this technique addicts are confronted about their manipulativeness, selfishness, dependency, and irresponsible behavior. As a result of my own experience in TCs, I am more con-
frontative in individual therapy sessions with addicts than any
other type of patient. In family sessions I am less confrontive in
order to avoid coalitions with the family against the patient.
However, if the patient is unwilling to participate in therapy,
then confrontation may motivate the patient to participate (see
Chapter 7).

The paradigm of confrontation is the "haircut." Here, several significant figures "take apart" a member. All of a person's
behavior is reviewed in a very brutal manner, although the
interaction is totally verbal. The individual is stripped of all of
sick patterns of behavior, followed by an attempt to "put the
person back together" by the end of the meeting. At some TCs
the hair is actually shaved off. Women's heads are generally not
shaved, but stocking caps are used. Presently, there is less
actual shaving of heads, with the procedure used mainly as a
last alternative to dismissal. An extreme of the "verbal haircut"
is the "fireplace ritual" in which individuals who have broken
cardinal rules and not reported them are ridiculed by the entire
community into revealing their "offense." Members confront
each other with their behavior and its impact on others until,
layer by layer, their defenses are removed. Marathons are also
utilized to break down defenses and lay individuals open to "the

gut level of emotional truth" (Rosenthal & Biase, 1969; Kaufman & DeLeon, 1978).

The Therapeutic Community Viewed as a Family

Synanon was founded on a family model and continues to recognize the need for strong paternal and maternal leaders. Most TC's are directed by strong, charismatic leaders. The prominent authorities of TCs are mainly nonprofessionals who have suffered exactly what the member has. In their identification with the therapists, the members feel that they are being told to do what is best for them and what they would do by themselves if they were not "babies." Thus the leaders of successful TCs are viewed as beloved but authoritarian parental figures.

Stratified Responsibility

This is an example of the "graduated gains of learning" theory, in which the individual accomplishes progressively more responsible tasks. At most TCs these levels are accomplished through the work necessary to maintain the house. Kitchen and service crews are of low status, building and administrative crews of moderate status, and those who acquire material goods and pursue community relations of higher status. Within each crew there is a hierarchy, with department heads assisted by "ramrods" followed by members. Still higher in status are expediters, chief expediter, and coordinator. Highest residential status is given to those with paid externships. These levels afford most residents their first opportunity to assume responsibility first for themselves and then for others. The numerous steps are necessary because the process of developing from follower to leader is a gradual one.

Acting "As If"

This is a technique with roots in AA, existentialism, and gestalt therapy, and it is so widely used in TCs that it deserves emphasis.

The principle of "as if" is simple: (1) first one sets a goal of the sort of person one would like to be; (2) next, one acts *as if* one actually were that person; (3) gradually, through the practice of acting that particular way, one actually changes in that direction. Even before any true change has occurred, people who are trying to stop abusing drugs or alcohol must perform "as if" change has already occurred (Casriel, 1963). They are asked to abstain from alcohol, drug use, lateness, and grossly inappropriate and antisocial behavior. They begin to abandon their self-destructive behaviors and to look for positive ways to live. Each step that is made in a positive direction is rewarded and acknowledged. As the time lengthens since the last negative act, the positive behavior is reinforced (Kaufman, 1973). Morning meetings, learning a new word or proverb every day, daily therapy groups, and regular marathon therapy sessions of 24 to 48 hours are also valuable therapeutic experiences used in TCs.

The technique of "as if" is also utilized in family therapy by Stuart (1980) in his "caring days" technique (see Chapter 8).

Results of Treatment in Therapeutic Communities

Although the proportion of entrants who graduate these long (as much as 18-months) programs is relatively low (about 10 percent; Glaser, 1974), time in treatment is generally correlated with positive psychological and social change, particularly among those who stay longer than 90 days (DeLeon, Rosenthal, & Brodney, 1971). One problem with all treatments for drug abuse is the lack of an aftercare system, as effective as AA that can be applied to the majority of drug abusers. Narcotics Anonymous (NA), based on principles similar to those of AA, has not been nearly as successful. One reason may be the chauvinism of the many different therapeutic communities and other treatment efforts for drug abuse; individuality has not permitted a united aftercare front, nor an association with so many treatment programs as has AA.

OTHER TREATMENT TECHNIQUES

Alcoholics Anonymous

Every successful treatment program for alcoholics I have been associated with has used AA principles as an integral part of the program, regardless of its orientation. The 12 steps of AA can be summarized in 5 principles: (1) admission of alcoholism and the total inability to drink, (2) dependence upon some higher power, (3) personality analysis and catharsis, (4) adjustment of personal relations, and (5) helping other alcoholics (Alibrandi, 1981). Attendance at large meetings only may be sufficient for many alcoholics to achieve rehabilitation. However, I find that actual work on the 12 steps is essential in most cases. This work can be facilitated by smaller study groups which specifically work on these steps. Although the vast majority of my successes have been greatly facilitated by AA, family treatment alone may be so effective that at times AA is not necessary, particularly if the alcoholic develops another successful system for abstaining from alcohol.

Hospital Treatment

Early treatment for drug dependence took place at federal drug treatment hospitals in Lexington, Kentucky, and Fort Worth, Texas, which opened in 1935 and 1938, respectively. During the first 30 years these hospitals were open there were about 100,000 admissions, including many returnees (National Commission on Marijuana and Drug Abuse, 1973). These federal facilities provided the major source of legal detoxification from opiates in the United States for three decades. Thus, many addicts regarded hospitalization as a necessary evil to keep their habit a manageable level, rather than as psychotherapy or an opportunity to change. Over half of all voluntary patients left Lexington before 30 days and another 22 percent left before the full period recommended by medical staff (usually 4 months). About 40 percent of patients were later readmitted to Lexington. Length of stay at Lexington was only "meagerly" associated with a lower admission rate (Ball, 1970). Vaillant (1966) performed a 12-year follow-up of a group of these addicts and found that 32 percent white, 28 percent black, and 20 percent hispanic addicts had maintained 3 years of abstinence. He also found that 24 percent of whites and 28 percent of blacks were deceased. That the results of the Lexington and Fort Worth experiences are not more favorable is a reflection of how difficult it is to treat unmotivated people.

From 1930 to 1960, drug-dependent persons were treated in state psychiatric hospitals, particularly in New York and California. These treatments tended to be short-term and met with limited success. In the early 1960s inpatient hospital detoxification from narcotics with the use of methadone became available at such centers as Manhattan General Hospital in New York City. The general experience with this modality was that almost half of the patients were unable to complete detoxification, and virtually all relapsed after returning to the street (Kaufman, 1978). In 1969, 96 patients were offered outpatient detoxification and a variety of treatments at Massachusetts General Hospital, but only two of these patients became engaged in treatment (Kaufman, 1975).

In 1961 California opened a series of "rehabilitation centers." Of 3300 addicts who left that program, only 300 were released due to successful completion of parole (Brecher, 1972).

Thus, early approaches to treating narcotic addiction were relative failures with the exception of about 30 percent of addicts who matured out. Newer approaches have been more successful, including the therapeutic community (described above), comprehensive outpatient programs, methadone maintenance, and narcotics antagonist programs.

The Outpatient Clinic

In "drug-free" mental health clinics, patients tend to be more motivated than typical methadone patients but less motivated than TC patients. A mental health clinic may also attract highly motivated patients with sufficient assets so that they do not require a TC to motivate them for intensive psychotherapy, nor do they require such a total treatment approach. Most of these patients can be treated successfully by one to two individual sessions weekly and one to five group sessions weekly, and they are able to continue their gains with individual or group sessions weekly to maintain support and therapist availability (Kaufman, 1978). These programs are more successful as they become more comprehensive. Thus, vocational programs and family therapy have begun to be added to individual and group therapy.

Methadone Maintenance and Narcotic Antagonist Programs

These programs can be valuable adjuncts to family treatment if the therapist has input into methadone dosage and if there is collaboration between the therapist and the program treatment team. As Stanton and Todd (1982) have noted, family therapy with patients in methadone maintenance works best when the family therapist has substantial input into determining methadone dose and detoxification. This diminishes the client's ability to manipulate and split the therapeutic team and permits the family therapist to work towards detoxification, a goal that is only achieved in about 10 percent of cases without family therapy (Kaufman, 1979). Both Stanton and Todd (1982) and Kaufman (1979) have noted that family therapy greatly enhances detoxification from methadone. However, in a chaotic, crisis-laden family with a narcotic addict, methadone maintenance may be essential to calming a family down to a point where family therapy can begin.

Narcotic antagonists such as naltrexone can also be used in the same way. Naltrexone blocks the effects of narcotics by competing for receptor sites, but unlike methadone it has no narcotic effect of its own. Thus, it requires a more highly motivated patient, but there is no physiologic withdrawal when the drug is discontinued.

Comprehensive Alcoholism Services

Alcoholism treatment services in general tend to be more comprehensive and integrated than drug abuse services. This may be related to the unifying principles of AA as well as to the better work record of many alcoholics, which permits them to afford private care. Private agencies are often willing to provide a wide range of reimbursable services. The available alcoholism services include information and referral centers, psychiatric hospitals, specialized hospitals for the treatment of alcoholism, alcoholism rehabilitation centers, aversive conditioning hospitals, shelters, halfway houses, and outpatient treatment programs. These will not be described in detail, as complete summaries of these programs are available (Pattison & Kaufman, 1982). The National Council of Alcoholism has more than 200 affiliates, with alcoholism information centers nationwide (Corrigan, 1980). In addition, most major treatment programs have information services, which include hotlines.

Psychiatric hospitals have long been a haven for alcoholics. When they treat alcoholics without specialized techniques and without implementing a system to achieve abstinence, the hospitals may serve as co-alcoholics, perpetuating alcoholism by inhibiting a commitment to sobriety. In general, alcoholics should not be treated as inpatients in a traditional psychiatric unit: Sociopathics, who constitute a minority of alcoholics, and antisocial substance abusers can manipulate a ward environment in a manner that prevents others from getting the treatment they need. Likewise, passive alcoholics can become dependent on inpatient treatment units or pass through without changing. "Bottomed-out" alcoholics may also pass through for "three hots and a cot" which keeps them alive but may ultimately keep them from the treatment they require.

Group Therapy

In order for the substance abuser to participate in group therapy, a contract is developed that limits continued misuse of drugs and alcohol (see Chapter 7). If this contract cannot be adhered to, admission to a detoxification center or hospital is recommended.

Early Phase

Group therapy should be started immediately after substance abuse stops or when detoxification is complete. At this time the client is so needy that resistance to groups is low. After a few days of sobriety defenses resolidify and therapy is resisted. Without alcohol or drugs to relieve life's problems, the client is depressed and frightened and desperately needs support. At this stage the therapist should help the client gain the attitude that a life without drugs is possible and better than life with drugs. In my experience, this type of technique is best done by a therapist, cotherapist who is a recovering alcoholic, or by an ex-addict, utilizing the techniques described earlier in this chapter.

There may, on the other hand, be a "honeymoon stage" after substance use stops, when all problems are denied and there is a sense of well-being. This lasts until the client realizes that the expected rewards of sobriety are not forthcoming.

During the early sessions of group therapy the focus is on the problem of drug and alcohol use and its meaning to each individual. The therapist should be more active during this phase, which should be instructional and informative as well as emotionally therapeutic (Fox, 1962). Alcoholics and drug abusers need to know a great deal about their condition, including definition, cause, symptoms, effects on bodily functions, and treatment. This may be done in a separate didactic experience or in the group. Didactic groups can be a good introduction to group therapy.

The desire to drink or use drugs and fear of slipping is a pervasive concern in the early phases of treatment. The patient's attitude is one of resistance, caution, and fear about openness and exploration. Members are encouraged to participate in AA, NA, or CA (Cocaine Anonymous), yet the high-support, low-conflict, inspirational style of these groups may inhibit interactional therapy. Therapists should not be overly protective and prematurely relieve the group's anxiety, as this fosters denial. On the other hand, the members' recognition of emotion and responsibility must proceed slowly, since both are particularly threatening to substance abusers.

In the early phases, I have found that these patients are superficially friendly, but do not show real warmth or tenderness. They are fearful of expressing anger or asserting themselves. However, sudden irritation, antipathy and anger with the leaders and other members inevitably begins to surface and must be dealt with carefully. Gradually tentative overtures of friendship and understanding become manifest (Fox, 1962). I have found that often there is a conspiracy of silence regarding any material which could cause discomfort and possible lead to "slips" (Brown & Yalom, 1977). The therapist can then point out to the members that they are choosing to remain static with comfortable limiting defenses rather than choosing the risks and discomfort associated with change. Patients may drop out early if they are still committed to drinking or drugs, or may grow more alarmed as they become aware of the degree of discomfort they will have to face to make significant changes. Fear of intimacy or of giving up longterm, vital, conflictual relationships also leads to early dropout (Kaufman, 1982).

Some substance abusers make confessionals or monologues about prior drinking or drug use. These can be politely interrupted or minimized by a ground rule entitled "no drunkalogues" or "no drugalogues."

Middle Phase

This phase may last from 6 months to several years. The client who successfully completes this phase will work through feelings, responsibility for behavior, interpersonal interactions, and the functions and secondary gains of substance-abusing behavior. He or she will become able to analyze defenses, resistance, and transference. The multiple transferences that develop in the group should be recognized as "old tapes," which are no longer relevant; problems of sibling rivalry, competition with authority figures, and separation anxiety become manifest in the group and are recognized as transferential. Conflicts are analyzed on both intrapsychic and interpersonal levels. Ventilation and catharsis take place and may be enhanced by role playing. There will be group identification and acceptance, as well as reality testing of old and new concepts and the abandonment of fantasy.

Substance abusers can be expected to show alternating cycles of improvement and retreat into former patterns of behavior, including drug use and drinking. Therapists should not be punitive about negative cycles, but neither should they condone drinking. The initial contract about AA, NA. or Antabuse can be reinforced when drinking or drug use reoccur. These cycles have a crisis flavor, and therapists should not participate in or contribute to these cycles by sharing defeat or undue optimism.

Alcohol and drug dependency conflicts may be expressed directly or covertly. Those who express dependency directly are better able to understand their dependency conflicts. However, in my experience their needs and frustrations are greater than in neurotic patients and when not met they repeatedly feel quite frustrated and disappointed. They demand praise, advice, and solutions; these should be offered initially and given less in the middle phases as they become capable of insight. The sick role may become an important source of identity and may be reinforced by the concept of alcoholism and drug use as a disease. This illness identity should be gradually relinquished since it lowers self-esteem. It should be replaced by taking responsibility for one's present counter-dependent behavior. Defenses such as a need to control or to deny feelings, are also gradually confronted and given up.

Alcoholics are often more ambivalent about positive feedback than are hardcore drug abusers. They beg for it, yet reject it when it is given. They repeatedly ask for physical reassurance but panic when they receive it because of their fear of intimacy and a reexperiencing of their unmet needs from the past. Rigidity and denial are greater in alcoholic groups than in any group except chronic schizophrenics. They are afraid to talk about unpleasant experiences because they are afraid they will be totally overwhelmed by all of their previous pain. They are reluctant to explore fantasies since the thoughts make them feel as guilty as the act. Consequently, they withhold critical comments because they fear criticism will provoke chaos and alcohol use in other members.

Most substance abusers fear success and dread competition in life and in the group. Success means destroying the other group members (siblings) and losing the therapist (parent). In contrast to former heroin addicts, alcoholics are frequently overly conscientious and assume blame and guilt for the emotional pain of other group members. Alcoholics tend to express rage either explosively or not at all. Its expression in group should be gradual; it can be facilitated by waiting until patients have good reason to be angry, and then challenging them. The challenge will add to the inner anger until nonverbal expression makes their anger clear to the group. Hard-core drug abusers, who are often more in touch with their anger, can easily be led by role-playing techniques to express anger in groups.

Role playing or doubling may facilitate expression of anger. In doubling, the therapist or another group member will sit behind the patient and express feelings which seem obvious yet are dammed up. When the patient finally expresses anger, he or she should be cheered and rewarded by the group with a hug or praise. Assertiveness training may increase a patient's ability to express and accept anger.

The other crucial affect to be dealt with in group therapy is depression. An initial severe depression may occur immediately after detoxification. This depression, which appears vegetative in its severity, usually remits rapidly, leaving a chronic, low-grade depression. Frequently depression is expressed by silence. These patients should be drawn out slowly and patiently and ultimately encouraged to cry or mourn. The "empty chair" technique may be used to facilitate mourning, including grief and anger towards lost love objects. The distinction must be made between helping patients deal with despair and rushing to take it away from them, as they must experience and live through depression if they are going to conquer it.

There is great resistance to open discussion of sexual issues in groups of alcoholics, and this topic should be gradually introduced by the therapist. Sexual issues are more easily discussed by drug abusers and addicts.

The success of the middle phase of group depends on the therapist's ability to relieve anxiety through group support, insight, and concrete methods, instead of through alcohol. In this vein, it is important to not end a session with members in a state of unresolved conflict. This can be avoided by bringing closure when troubling issues are raised, which can be achieved by asking the group for concrete suggestions to resolve problems. When this is not possible group support, including extra group contact by members, can be offered.

Closing Phase

By the time alcoholics and drug abusers have reached this phase, they have achieved the same level of group function as purely neurotic patients. Thus, substance abusers in this phase are working on their underlying neurotic core (Fox, 1982). Alcoholics and prescription drug abusers who survive a high initial drop-out rate stay in groups longer than neurotic patients, and many will reach this phase (Kaufman, 1982). By now the clients have accepted sobriety without resentment and have developed a healthy self-concept and empathy for others. They have scaled down their inordinate demands on others, and are effectively assertive rather than destructively aggressive. They have developed a reasonable sense of values and achieved fulfilling relationships with spouses, children, and friends.

The decision to leave the group should be discussed for several weeks before a final date is set. This permits mutual mourning of loss. This is true regardless of the stage of the group, but more intense work on termination is done in later phases. In open-ended groups, the leadership qualities of the graduating member are taken over by remaining members, who may in turn transfer these leadership qualities to their lives outside the group.

Since many substance abusers may be in group and individual treatment with ex-addicts, recovering alcoholics, and other therapists using these modalities, it is important that family therapists be familiar with the techniques discussed in this chapter. In addition, many of these techniques and principles can be incorporated into the family therapy of substance abusers. I had been pleased with the success of these methods over a fifteen-year period but my success rate improved dramatically when family techniques were incorporated into my therapeutic approach as described in the chapters that follow.

————————————————————————————— REFERENCES

Alibrandi, L. The fellowship of Alcoholics Anonymous. In E.M. Pattison & E. Kaufman (Eds.), *Encyclopedic handbook of alcoholism.* 1982, 979–986. Gardner Press, N.Y.

Ball, J.C. Readmission rates at Lexington Hospital for 43,215 narcotic drug addicts. *Public Health Report,* 1970, 85, 610.

Brecher, E.M. and Consumer Reports Editors. *Licit and illicit drugs: The Consumer's Union report on narcotics, stimulants, depressants, inhalents, hallucinogens, and marijuana—including caffeine, nicotine, and alcohol.* Waltham, Mass.: Little Brown, 1972.

Brown, S., & Yalom, I.D. Interactional Group Therapy with alcoholics. *Journal of Studies on Alcohol,* 1977, 38:426–456.

Casriel, D. *So fair a House: The story of Synanon.* Englewood Cliffs, N.J.: Prentice-Hall, 1963.

Corrigan, E.M. *Alcoholic women in treatment.* New York/Oxford, Oxford University Press, 1980.

DeLeon, G., Rosenthal, M.S., & Brodney, K. Therapeutic community for drug addicts: Long-term measurements of emotional changes, *Psychological Report,* 1971, 29, 595.

Fox, R. Group psychotherapy with alcoholics. *International journal of group psychotherapy* 1962, 12:56–63.

Glaser, F.B. Guadenzia, Inc., Historical and theoretical background on a self-help addiction treatment program. *International Journal of Addiction,* 1971, 6(4), 615.

Glaser, F.B. Some historical aspects of the drug-free therapeutic community. *American Journal of Drug and Alcohol Abuse,* 1974, 1(1), 37–52.

Glaser, F.B. Splitting: Attribution from a drug-free therapeutic community. *American Journal of Drug and Alcohol Abuse,* 329–348, 1974, 1(3).

Jones, M. *Social psychiatry in practice.* Harmondsworth, England: Penguin, 1968.

Kaufman, E., Group therapy techniques used by the ex-addict therapist. *Group Process,* 1973, 5, 3–19.

Kaufman, E., Psychiatric approaches to drug dependence. In A. Schecter (Ed.), *Treatment aspects of drug dependence.* Fla.: CRC Press, 1978, 109–116.

Kaufman, E. The therapeutic community and methadone: A way of achieving abstinence, *International Journal of the Addiction,* West Palm Beach, Fla.: CRC Press, 1979, 14(1), 83–97.

Kaufman, E., & DeLeon, G. The therapeutic community: A treatment approach for drug abusers. In A. Schecter (Ed.), *Treatment aspects of drug dependence.* West Palm Beach, Fla.: CRC Press, 1978, 83–97.

Kaufman, E. Group therapy for substance abusers, Grotjahn, M., Friedman, C., & Kline, F. (Eds.), *A handbook of group therapy,* New York, N.Y.: Van Nostrand, 1982, 163–191.

Leach, B., Norris, J.L., Dancey, T., & Bissell, L. Dimensions of Alcoholics Anonymous: 1935–1965. *International Journal of Addictions,* 1969, 4, 507.

National Commission on Marijuana and Drug Abuse. *Drug use in America: Problem in Perspective (2nd report)*. Washington, D.C.: U.S. Government Printing Office, 1973.

Rosenthal, M.S., & Biase, D.V. Phoenix House's therapeutic communities for drug addicts. *Hospital Community Psychiatry*, 43, 1969.

Stanton, E.D., Todd, T.C. *The family therapy of drug abuse and addiction*. New York, London: Guilford Press, 1982.

Stuart, R.B. *Helping couples change*, New York, Guilford Press, 1980.

Vaillant, G.E. A 12-year follow-up of New York narcotic addicts: III. Some social and psychiatric characteristics, *Archives of General Psychiatry*, 1966, *15*, 599.

Wilson, B. *Alcoholics Anonymous comes of age: A brief history of A.A.* New York: *Alcoholics Anonymous World Services*, 1957.

General Principles in Family Treatment of Substance Abusers

The cornerstone of family treatment of substance abuse is developing a system to achieve and maintain abstinence. This system, together with specific family therapeutic techniques, which will be described in the chapters that follow and knowledge of the family patterns that have been described previously, will provide therapeutic satisfaction for the therapist and meaningful, helpful change for families.

ASSESSMENT OF THE EXTENT OF SUBSTANCE ABUSE

It is important that in the first session the therapist evaluate the extent of substance abuse/dependence as well as the difficulties it presents for the individual and family. I generally take this history with the entire family present, as I find that substance abusers often will be honest in this setting and "confession" is a helpful way to begin communication. On the other hand, other family members can often provide more accurate information than the substance abuser (also known as the *identified patient* or IP), and some IPs will give an accurate history only when interviewed alone. In taking a drug abuse history it is important to know what use has been of every type of abusable drug as well as alcohol: quantity, quality, duration, expense, how intake was supported and prevented, physical effects, tolerance, withdrawal, and medical complications. It is only when the use of alcohol and other drugs is documented thoroughly that the specific system necessary to achieve abstinence can be decided upon.

EARLY ESTABLISHMENT OF A SYSTEM FOR DEVELOPING A SUBSTANCE-FREE STATE

It is critical to establish a system for enabling the substance abuser to become sober, so that family therapy can take place effectively. The specific methods employed to achieve abstinence vary according to the extent of use, abuse, and dependence. Mild to moderate abuse in adolescents can often be controlled if both parents can agree on clear limits and expectations and how to enforce them. Older abusers may also stop if they are made aware of the medical or psychological consequences to themselves or the effects on their family.

If substance abuse is moderately severe or intermittent and without physical dependence, such as binge alcoholism or weekend cocaine abuse, then the family is offered a variety of measures to initiate a substance-free state, including, social detoxification centers, regular attendance at Alcoholics Anonymous (AA), Narcotics Anonymous (NA), or Cocaine Anonymous (CA), and Antabuse (disulfiram) for alcoholics. Heroin addicts can be detoxified on an outpatient basis with clonidine or methadone, the latter only in specialized 21-day programs. Some mild to moderate substance abusers who are resistant to self-help groups may find that another system helps them stay off of drugs (religion, exercise regime, relaxation technique, career change).

As abuse progresses, more aggressive methods are necessary to establish a substance-free system. If the abuser's intake is so severe that he or she is unable to attend sessions sober, if social or vocational functioning is severely impaired, if there is drug-related violence, and/or if there is physical dependence, then the first priority in treatment is to stop substance use immediately. This involves persuading the family to pull together to achieve at least temporary abstinence. Generally, this is best done in a hospital. Thus, if the abuse pattern is severe, hospitalization will be set as a requirement very early in therapy.

ESTABLISHING A SYSTEM FOR MAINTAINING A SUBSTANCE FREE STATE

The family is urged to adopt some system that will enable the abuser to continue to stay free of alcohol and other abuse substances. This system is part of the therapeutic contract made early in treatment. A lifetime committment to abstinence is not required. Rather, the "one day at a time" approach of AA is recommended; the patient is asked to establish a system for abstinence, which is committed to for only one day at a time but which is renewed daily using the basic principles of AA, NA, or CA.

I tell each new family that therapy is generally quite successful when all family members work toward abstinence and that it almost never works (at least with me as the therapist) if controlled drinking or substance use is the goal. For one thing, the individual cannot fully utilize CA, AA, or NA as a support group while abusing any substance. I also inform the family that the vast majority of individuals who have lost control of any drug or alcohol in their past are very poor candidates for controlled use of potentially abusable substances at any later time in their lives.

Many individuals have to shop for an AA group in which they feel personally comfortable. Every recovering alcoholic is strongly encouraged to attend small study groups, which work on the 12 steps, as well as larger "open" meetings, which often have speakers and which anyone can attend.

Anatabuse should generally not be given to a family member for daily distribution to the alcoholic (with the exception of type I, stable families), as it tends to reinforce the family's overinvolvement in the alcoholic's drinking or not drinking. Benzodiazepines are discouraged for outpatients because they tend to become part of the problem rather than part of a solution. Some heroin addicts will do quite well on methadone maintenance or naltrexone antagonist therapy, particularly when used in conjunction with family therapy. An ultimate goal with almost every methadone maintenance client in family therapy is a totally drug-free state.

The ability of former alcoholics to drink in a controlled manner is still a subject of great controversy. There is some recent evidence that about 3 percent of former alcoholics are able to do so (Pettinati, Sugarman, DiDonato, & Maurer, 1982). Some studies show a higher incidence of controlled drinking. These results may be either because of inadequate longterm follow-up or because of a sample comprised of people who were not truly alcoholic or who were dependent on alcohol for only a short period of time (Vaillant, 1983). Alcoholics who have had prior extended periods of controlled drinking and social stability may be better able to achieve controlled drinking than those who have not.

In my experience, treatment is often much more effective if the patient is totally immersed in a 28-day residential treatment program that includes detoxification, individual and group therapy, AA/CA/NA, and family therapy. Short-term (28-day) programs have a very high success rate with alcoholics, particularly those who commit themselves to AA.

This type of intense treatment may by itself provide the impetus for even a non-addicted, occasional drug user to get off and stay off of drugs, particularly if there is effective, comprehensive aftercare. Individuals who have been dependent on illicit drugs for more than a few years generally do not do well in short-term programs, although these programs may buy time so that effective individual and family therapy can occur. For many drug-dependent patients, insistence on long-term residential treatment is the only workable alternative. Most families, however, will not accept this until other methods have failed. In order to accomplish this end a therapist must be willing to maintain longterm ties with the family, even through multiple treatment failures. On the other hand, it may be more helpful to terminate treatment if the substance abuser continues to abuse chemicals, as continued family treatment implies that change is occurring when it is not. One way to continue therapist-family ties while not condoning substance abuse is to work with the family without the substance abuser present (this will be described below). In other cases it is more effective to terminate treatment until all family members are willing and able to adopt a workable system for reinforcing abstinence. Families that truly believe I am terminating in their best interest almost always return a few months or years later, ready and willing to commit to abstinence.

A summary of the measures available to establish and/or maintain a substance abuse free state is presented in Table 7-1. This table demonstrates the flexibility in approach necessary to accomplish this and how it varies with extent and type of substance abuse.

FAMILY TREATMENT DURING
CONTINUED SUBSTANCE ABUSE

Bowen (1974) and Berenson (1979) have developed treatment approaches for working with families while a member continues to drink problematically. However, I know of no successful programs for working with the families of presently addicted drug abusers, although it is possible theoretically that this could be done by first changing family structures through restructuring techniques. Berenson (1979) offered a series of steps and chores for the non-alcoholic spouse which I have found clinically useful, particularly when the drinking member refuses to enter or return to treatment: (1) Calm down the family system and porvide clarity (e.g., by explaining problems and solutions). (2) Create a support system for family members so that the emotional intensity isn't all within the session or in the relationships with the alcoholic. In Al-Anon, the group and/ or the sponsor may provide emotional support and calm down the situation. Steps 1 and 2 may also be facilitated by having the spouses/significant others (SOs) of the alcoholic participate together in a group, in addition to or in place of Al-Anon. This group provides support to the SOs, and frequently, after several months, the alcoholic may join the partner in a couples group. Step 3 involves giving the spouse three choices: (a) keep doing exactly what you are doing, (b) detach or emotionally distance yourself from the alcoholic, or (c) separate or physically distance yourself. When the client does not change, it is labelled an overt

Table 7-1
THE UTILIZATION OF MEASURES TO ESTABLISH AND MAINTAIN A SUBSTANCE ABUSE FREE STATE

	"Recreational" Drug and Alcohol Abuse	Substance Abuse Opiates, Stimulants, Hallucinogens, Sedative-Hypnotics, Alcohol, Minor Tranquilizers, Inhalents	Binge Alcoholism, Severe Self-Destructive Drug Related Behaviors	Drug Dependence Inhalents, Cocaine, Amphetamines, Hallucinogens	Drug Dependence Opiates	Drug Dependence Alcohol, Sedative-Hypnotics, Minor Tranquilizers
Hospitalize (28 days)	*	**	***	**	**	***
Out-patient detox				***	***	***
AA, NA, or CA	**	**	***	***	**	***
Family therapy	**	***	***	***	***	***
Long-term residence		*	*	**	***	
Antabuse			**			**
Methadone maintenance					**	
Relaxation techniques	**	**	**	**	**	**
Group therapy	**	**	**	**	**	**

Mandatory *** Recommended ** Optional *

110

choice (a). When a client does not choose (b) or (c), the therapist can point out that he or she is in effect choosing (a). In choice (b) spouses are helped to not criticize drinking, to accept it, to live with the alcoholic, and to be responsible for their own reactivity regarding drinking.

Although each of these choices may seem impossible to carry out, the problem is usually resolved by choosing one and following through, often only after experiencing the helplessness and powerlessness of these situations being repeated and clarified. As part of the initial contract with a couple, I request that the abuser's partner commit to continue individual treatment, Al-Anon, and/or a spouse group *even if* the abuser drops out. Other family members are also encouraged to continue in family therapy and support groups. It should be reemphasized that whenever we maintain therapy with a "wet" alcoholic or drup abuser, we have the responsibility of *not* maintaining the illusion that a family is resolving problems while in fact it is really reinforcing them.

Another method for dealing with treatment-resistant drinking alcoholics is "The Intervention," developed at the Johnson Institute in Minnesota and the Freedom Institute in New York (1980). In this technique, the family (excluding the abuser), and significant network members including employer, fellow employees, friends, and neighbors are coached to confront the alcoholic, with concern but without hostility, about the destructiveness of his or her drinking and behavior. They agree in advance about what treatment is necessary and then insist on it. As many family members as possible should be included, as the breakthrough for acceptance of treatment may come from an apparently uninvolved family member such as a grandchild or cousin. The involvement of the employer is crucial, and in some cases may be sufficient in and of itself to motivate the alcoholic to seek treatment. The employer who clearly makes treatment a precondition of continued employment, who supports time off for treatment, and who guarantees a job upon completion of the initial treatment is a very valuable ally. This paradigm explains the very high success rate of industrial alcoholism treatment.

Several techniques and attitudes will help get reluctant family members into therapy. Obviously critical to getting any family into treatment is knowing what to do with the entire family when it arrives. Once the family therapist has a knowledge of the substance abusing family, a system for dealing with substance abuse, and a workable personal system of family therapy, it becomes remarkably easy to get the entire family to come in for treatment.

A major issue in getting total families into therapy is the policy of the clinic or therapist about families, as well as the attitude of the individual who handles the first telephone contact with families. It is important that the contact person informs the family that everyone in the family is expected to come in. This approach will provide a great deal of momentum towards the entire family participating from the onset of treatment. However, the therapist should be flexible enough to be willing to see a family without all members present in the very first interview(s). This is also true for a family with a reluctant alcoholic who requires an intervention or the spouse who requires a significant others group or other individual program.

With these exceptions in mind, the general policy should be that therapy can only begin when all family members are present. Seeing the identified patient alone at the onset of treatment risks reinforcing the idea that he or she is *the* problem, increases scapegoating, and continues family resistance to full participation in therapy (Bauman, 1981). One the other hand, seeing the family without the IP sets up coalitions that increase the abuser's hostility to therapy and alienation, although this may be necessary when an intervention is indicated.

Initial resistance to the suggestion that all family members attend the first interview may come from the family member who called for help or from other family members. If the resistance is from the caller, then issues such as time problems, fear of hurting family members, or concerns about family secrets need to be dealt with supportively (Bauman, 1981). If the caller states that other members do not want to be involved, this may be due to the caller's need to protect others from therapy or the caller's fear of consequences if certain members attend. These fears may be briefly explored and the responsiblility of the caller to bring everyone in for therapy to succeed emphasized.

It is best if the caller alone rallies the entire family, but in some cases the therapist may have to contact one or more family members directly. If a reluctant family member claims to no longer be involved with the family, the therapist can truthfully point out that he or she would be valuable because of objectivity. If the member says his or her relationship with the family is too painful, then the therapist can emphasize the potential helpfulness to that person of joining therapy. The therapist may emphasize his or her own inability to help the family unless that member attends. Reluctant family members can also be asked to attend to protect their interests, to prevent a skewed view and ensure that all views are delineated, to preserve fairness, and even to come just without any obligation to participate. Most family members will agree to a single evaluative visit. It then becomes imperative for the therapist to establish a contract with the family that all members feel will relieve their pains as well as that of the IP. Not infrequently, however, some will not show up. The therapist may deal with this by cancelling the session, which gives a strong message that the whole family needs to attend. I prefer to hold a brief session that deals only with the strategies necessary to get the absent members in. At times this may require an extended availability on the part of the therapist but once the family is involved in treatment they may become more flexible.

Stanton and Todd (1982) have been successful in getting 70 percent of the families of methadone maintenance patients—a generally unreachable group—into an initial interview. Ninety-four percent of these who attended the initial session continued with treatment. Stanton and Todd presented 21 valuable, basic, facilitatory principles, which include (1) the therapist delivering a non-blaming message that focuses on helping the patient rather than the family. (2) "The rationale for family treatment should be presented in such a way that, in order to oppose it, family members would have to state openly that they want to index patient to remain symptomatic." (3) "The program must be structured in a way that does not allow the therapist to back down from enlisting whole families" (Stanton & Todd, 1982).

The concept of the family as a multigenerational system necessitates that the entire family be involved in treatment. In my experience, family therapy limited to any diad is most difficult. The mother–addicted son diad is almost impossible to treat, and someone else must be brought in if treatment is to succeed. If there is absolutely no one elso available, surrogate family members in multiple family therapy provide leverage to facilitate restructuring maneuvers (Kaufman and Kaufmann, 1977).

Therapy limited to alcoholism, all to often has excluded the crucial parents or progeny of the alcoholic. Children are not just victims of alcoholic families. By their reciprocating involvement in these systems, they contribute to the problem and are a necessary part of the solution, regardless of age.

Treatment for drug addicts and their spouses has been less effective treatment for alcoholic couples. This led Stanton and Todd (1982) to suggest that family treatment of male narcotic addicts begin with their parents, and that the addict–spouse couple should not be worked with until the addict's parents can "release" him to his spouse. Phoenix House has found so much difficulty with addicted couples that they insist on separate residential treatment sites for such couples. At a therapeutic community at Metropolitan State Hospital in California (The Awakening Family), we have met with some success with treating addicted couples in the same program. Success is enhanced by insisting on couple therapy throughout their stay in the program. Another essential aspect of treating couples with children is focusing on their functions as parents, and therapy involving children has the distinct advantage of developing parenting skills. Thus, I strongly advise the utilization of a multigenerational approach involving grandparents, parents, spouse, and children. When most other family problems are resolved a couples group can be very helpful, but it should never be the sole modality of family therapy, which it is in so many treatment programs.

AN INTEGRATED APPROACH TO TREATMENT

There is a need for an integrated approach that utilizes other techniques in addition to family therapy. My family approach with drug addicts and abusers would be relatively ineffective without methadone, propoxyphene, or clonidine detoxification; methadone and L-alpha-acetyl-methadol (LAAM) maintenance, naltrexone; residential therapeutic communities; hospital detoxification; Narcotics Anonymous; specialized vocational rehabilitation; individual and group psychotherapy, particularly the techniques of ex-addicts; and so on. Similarly, with alcoholics, I would feel powerless without AA, Al-Anon, Alateen, Antabuse, specialized residential treatment, and the availability of medication when needed to treat underlying affective and psychotic disorders. Thus I use an integrated, multidisciplinary approach which meets each patient's needs and is directed toward solving individual problems.

These general principles are built into the contract with the family, which is developed at the end of the first or second session. They include the following:

1. A support system such as AA, NA, or CA to reinforce abstinence.
2. Refusal to treat until the family accepts a system that will stop substance abuse, including hospitalization when necessary.
3. Pharmacotherapy of underlying diagnosable psychiatric problems, using drugs of little or no abuse potential, like tricyclic antidepressants or lithium, not benzodiazepines or sedative–hypnotics.
4. Insistence that the entire family participate in therapy.
5. Al-Anon or a significant others groups for the spouse, Alateen or other group for the children.
6. Therapeutic work with the spouse if the drug-abusing partner does not stop. This therapy should consist of a support group as well as individual psychotherapy.
7. A choice of drug-free relaxation techniques, including self-hypnosis, bio-feed back, yoga, meditation, and aerobic exercise.

--- REFERENCES

Bauman, M.H. Involving resistant family members in therapy, In A. Gurman (Ed.), *Questions and answers in the practice of family therapy.* New York: Guilford, 1981, 16–19.

Berenson, D. The therapist's relationship with couples with an alcoholic member. In E. Kaufman & P. Kaufmann (Eds.), Family therapy of drug and alcohol abuse. New York: Gardner Press, 1979, 233–242.

Bowen, M. Alcoholism as viewed through family systems theory and family psychotherapy. Annals of the New York Academy of Science, 1974, 233, 115–122.

Freedom Institute, 11 East 74th St, New York, New York, 10021. In Mimeo, 1980.

Kaufman, E., & Kaufmann, P. Multiple family therapy: A new direction in the treatment of drug abusers. American Jouranl of Drug and Alcohol Abuse, 1977, 4, 467–478.

Pettinati, H.M., Sugarman, A.A., DiDonato, M.A., & Maurer, H.S. The natural history of alcoholism over four years after treatment. Journal of Studies on Alcohol, 1982, 43, (3), 201–215.

Stanton, M.D., & Todd, T.C. The family therapy of drug abuse and addiction. New York: Guilford, 1982.

Vaillant, G.E. The natural history of alcoholism. Cambridge, Mass.: Harvard University Press, 1983.

Part IV

FAMILY TREATMENT
TECHNIQUES

Chapter 8

A Review of Family Therapy Techniques with Substance Abusers

Every system of family therapy that has evolved over the past two decades can be applied to substance abusers if the therapist has a knowledge of substance abuse (Chapter 1) the specific family systems (Chapters 2–5), other treatment techniques (Chapter 6), and the general principles of family treatment of substance abusers (Chapter 7). These other systems of family therapy are described in innumerable books and journal articles on the subject and are well summarized in the *Handbook of Family Therapy* edited by Gurman and Kniskern (1981). This anthology characterizes the different types of family therapy into four basic categories: psychoanalytic and object relations, intergenerational, systems, and behavioral. However, Gurman and Kniskern, like others in this field, have noted the tremendous overlap between approaches, since all family therapists look at the family as a system and are problem-focused. They use the term "pragmatic psychodynamics" to describe this commonality of approaches. In pragmatic psychodynamic family therapy, dynamic principles are acknowledged and accepted but are utilized in a general systems framework rather than a psychoanalytic framework, to select those techniques and strategies that are most likely to resolve family problems in a rapid fashion. [The term "pragmatic psychodynamic" was of interest

119

to me as it was one which I had coined earlier as the title of a course I taught in 1978—"Pragmatic Psychodynamic Psychotherapy." The course consisted of the utilization of psychodynamic principles to achieve "here and now" change in individual psychotherapy. Pragmatic utilization of psychodynamic principles also influenced by work with families (see Chapter 9).]

All therapy should be pragmatic, that is, aimed toward getting things done. No system in and of itself is more pragmatic than any other, but depends on the ability of the individual therapist to incorporate it into a personal style and effectively apply it to patients and families.

Each of the systems of family therapy presently in use will be summarized in this chapter, with an emphasis on those practitioners who have specifically applied their techniques to substance abusers. I have classified the schools of family therapy into structural–strategic, psychodynamic, Bowen's systems theory, and behavioral groupings.

STRUCTURAL–STRATEGIC THERAPY

These two types are combined because they were developed by the same practitioners, and shifts between the two are frequently made by these therapists depending on the family's needs. Family structure refers to the invisible set of functional demands that organizes interaction among family members. The goal of structural family therapy (SFT) is a more adequate family organization achieved through manipulation and rearrangement of present patterns of interaction (Minuchin, 1974). Boundaries are rules defining who participates in the family and how. These may be represented as follows:

—— —— —— ——	clear
. . . .	diffuse
———————————————	rigid

Subsystems may be formed by generation, sex, interest, or function. The two most common subsystems are executive (parental) and sibling. The relationships between family members may be designated as shown below:

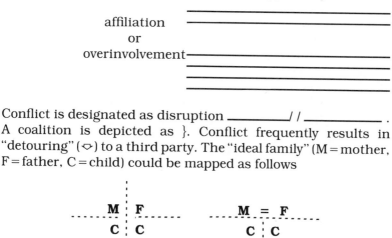

affiliation
or
overinvolvement

Conflict is designated as disruption _____/ /_____ .
A coalition is depicted as }. Conflict frequently results in
"detouring" (♡) to a third party. The "ideal family" (M = mother,
F = father, C = child) could be mapped as follows

with clear boundaries between all individuals, affiliation between
parents, and separation of the executive and sibling subsystems. The spouse subsystem must have sufficient complementarity and mutual accommodation to implement tasks. The child
should have access to both parents but be excluded from spousal
functions. Parents cannot protect and guide without controlling
and restricting, just as children cannot grow and become individuated without rejecting and attacking (Minuchin, 1974).

Stanton (1981) summarized the basic similarities of and
differences between structural (SFT) and strategic family therapy and proposed a system for integrating these approaches "in
a concurrent and contrapuntal fashion." The thrust of structural family therapy is to restructure the system by creating
interactional change within the session. The therapist actively
becomes a part of the family, yet retains sufficient autonomy to
restructure the family (Stanton, 1981). (The techniques of SFT
are described in detail in Chapter 9.)

According to strategic therapists, symptoms are maladaptive attempts to deal with difficulties, which develop a homeostatic life of their own and continue to regulate family transactions. The strategic therapist works to substitute new behavior
patterns for the destructive repetitive cycles. The techniques
used by strategic therapists include the following, which are
explained later in this chapter (Stanton, 1981):

1. Using Primary tasks and directives
2. Putting the problem in measurable and solvable form
3. Placing considerable emphasis on change outside the sessions
4. Learning to take the path of least resistance, so that power struggles are avoided and the family's existing behaviors are used positively
5. Use of paradox, including restraining change and exaggerating the family's position.

Madanes (1981) cited the following additional common features of strategic therapy:

1. The responsiblility is on the therapist to plan a strategy for solving the client's problems.
2. The therapist intervenes with the family so that the presenting problem is no longer necessary.
3. Change occurs in stages. (a) The therapist may create a new problem so that solving it leads to solving the original problem. (b) The family heirarchy may be shifted to a different, abnormal one before reorganizing it into a new functional heirarchy.
4. Use of metaphorical directives in which the family does not know they have received a directive.
5. If a strategy doesn't work, change it.

Hoffman (1981) noted that in strategic therapy, family subgroups are seen more than the entire family, and at times one subgroup may be pitted against the other. She suggested that in utilizing the strategic approach, the therapist must understand how a symptom is reframed positively by emphasizing how it serves a "helpful" function to the system, and the symptom should be encouraged to be continued since it is so important to the family. Hoffman warned that the strategic approach may be hazardous to beginners because it is deceptively simple. I feel that strategic techniques have been glorified of late, while more directive approaches have been denigrated. Strategic therapy should not be utilized until the therapist has first mastered a more directive approach such as SFT. In addition, this technique should not be used unless directive techniques are not working or a specific family pattern such as a symptom-focused repetitive cycle calls for strategic intervention.

Strategic therapy makes covert behaviors into overt actions, frequently through the use of paradoxes (Haley, 1977). In utilizing the paradox, the therapist's intent is to have the family follow the implied covert message, which is the opposite of the stated overt message. The paradox works on the principle of the double bind, so that the family must be first joined to the therapist (unable to leave the field). The paradox is delivered at the end of the session so that, as with the double bind, the patient or family cannot comment on or dispute the message. There are four basic types of paradoxes (1) "reframing" or giving the symptom a new, frequently positive meaning, (2) redirecting or changing the circumstances under which a symptom occurs, (3) inducing or escalating a crisis to shift a rigid system, and (4) restraining the family from changing too fast.

Stanton (1981) offered a relevant example of redirection in dealing with a parent's secretly providing drugs to a drug-abusing child. He suggested that a contract be negotiated as to how much drug use should be allowed, when drugs are given, and who should distribute the drugs. The same paradox can be used to make explicit a parent's provision of money for drugs or for lawyers and bail when done on the sly to not —"worry" the other parent or protect the drug abuser from the other parent's anger. This is also an example of helping the family to control symptoms by redirecting or prescribing them when they occur rather than having the symptoms control the family. Another example of paradox is to positively reframe and prescribe the behavior of each family member which perpetuates the dysfunctional system (Stanton (1981), Pallozzoli et al. (1980).

In utilizing the restraining mode of paradox, the therapist discourages change, denies that change is possible, emphasizes the dangers of improvement or tells the family to slow down because they are changing faster than they can tolerate (Stanton, 1981).

Papp (1980) described three steps in utilizing a paradox. First, define the symptoms as being benignly motivated to protect the family. Second, prescribe the symptom producing cycle of interaction and finally, restrain the family from changing. (See Chapter 9 for further discussion of paradox.)

Stanton (1980) provided rules for using structural and strategic approaches concurrently or alternatively. He suggested that the therapist initially deal with a family through a structural approach, switching to a strategic approach when structural techniques are unlikely to succeed or are not working. Following success with strategic methods, Stanton suggests that the therapist switch again to a structural approach when the IP has become less central and structural techniques such as marking boundaries and strengthening spousal bonds are more appropriate.

Strategic therapists avoid power struggles, choosing instead to travel the path of least resistance (Stanton, 1981). One example of this is the "gossiping" technique developed by Palazzoli et al. (1980), in which a family member is asked to talk about the interaction or relationship between two other family members so that those two don't have to continue to attack each other. Haley (Hoffman, 1981) suggested providing an illusion of alternatives (would you like to do this task on Thursday or Saturday) or providing a worse alternative so that the client utilizes a different but effective method. He may even use a "devil's pact" in which the family agrees to the directive before they hear it.

PSYCHODYNAMIC THERAPY

This approach has rarely been applied to substance abusers because they usually require a more active, limit-setting emphasis on the here and now than is usually associated with psychodynamic techniques.

Psychodynamic family therapy has come a long way from Ackerman's initial constructs, which urged the therapist to strip away the defense mechanisms of each family member so that the underlying conflicts become clear. Nevertheless, Ackerman was probably the first to state that family treatment focused on the behavior disorders of a system of interacting personalities—the family group (Ackerman, 1970).

The basic principles of the psychodynamic approach are, first, using history to uncover past actions which are inappropriately applied to the present (transference) and, second, creating change through insight. This insight is achieved by cognitive or affective re-encounter with the past (Kaufman, 1979) and, in a strict psychodynamic framework, must precede change. (See Chapter 9 for further detail on my use of psychodynamic therapy in treating substance abusers.)

Group Analytic Approach

Skynner (1976, 1981) espouses a "group-analytic" approach to family therapy. He sees families as suffering from developmental failures, which are passed on from one generation to the next. Each partner brings to the family expectations and fears corresponding to the level at which their own developmental process was blocked. These fears are projected onto the members of their nuclear family. Thus, Skynner feels that therapy requires identification of these projective systems, followed by bringing them back into the marriage where they can be dealt with constructively. He suggests that "well" siblings may be sicker than the IP because they have more rigid defenses and may not be as open to growth. He classifies therapeutic intervention as "from above," "from the side," and "from below." In acting "from above," the therapist is authoritative and directive and changes the family by active intervention, advice, instruction, praise, criticism, education, or modeling. In intervention from "the side," a detached therapist outwits the family at their own manipulative methods of control to achieve desired structural change. Therapists who operate "from below" appear to submit to the control of the family but are detached enough to comment on their process; the therapist can confront the family yet keep the responsibility on the family to change. Skynner, like most family therapists, regardless of their "official" orientation, operates alternately from all three levels, depending on the family's needs.

One example of Skynner's analytic orientation is that he feels the real family problem "is always contained in what is not communicated" and is missing from the overt content of the session. Another example is that he feels that the therapist needs to maintain an awareness of self-identity throughout encounters with a disturbed family system "seeking to externalize their pathology" (countertransference awareness). He emphasizes that insight may follow change but that change also follows insight. Nevertheless, Skynner also marks intergenerational boundaries, clarifies communication, and teaches new skills, as do most family therapists regardless of orientation. Each person is helped to be separate and independent and not "need" the other.

Family of Origin Technique

Framo (1981) is also frequently associated with the psychodynamic movement and one of his major contributions is quite helpful with the families of substance abusers. He has suggested that "family of origin" (F of O) work (including parents and siblings) be done with adult patients in addition to work with the nuclear family. Framo informs each spouse that he will eventually meet with them and their own family of origin without their spouse being present. He takes a brief history of the family of origin and present relationships with parents and siblings. Because of a high level of anxiety about such meetings, the F of O session takes place towards the end of therapy. During the early work with couples, Framo occasionally asks direct questions of a person about what is going on between them and their parents and siblings (Framo, 1976, 1981). As therapy progresses he notes that marital conflicts fade in importance and are replaced with the need to work out a better relationship with the F of O. Each client develops a list of critical issues to be brought up with every member of the family. Spouses are generally quite supportive of each other working things out with F of O (Framo, 1981).

The actual F of O session is a very valuable tool during which underlying positive feelings are drawn out as well as negative ones. The session deals with happy memories, tragedies, roles, and alliances in order to help achieve an understanding of how past family problems are being lived through the present (Framo, 1976). This powerful four-hour session is recorded so that all absent members (every effort is made to have everyone attend) as well as those present can review and integrate this material. These F of O sessions serve to demythologize the F of O as well as transference distortions in the marriage (Framo, 1980). I have found F of O work to be very helpful with substance-abusing families who are stuck in what Framo (1976) termed the "dirty middle" of therapy, where no one is willing to take the responsibility for change because of strong intrapsychic needs. F of O oriented therapy may also help uncover the hidden agenda of the marriage, which needs to be dealt with to get families unstuck from circular repetitive processes.

Framo's F of O therapy differs from Bowenian strategies in that there are no timed visits to families, no extended genogram work, and no coaching to control emotional reactivity. The therapist is present for all of the family interactions, which usually are highly changed emotionally. Although Framo objects to being called psychoanalytic, he accepts the notions that "what goes on inside people's heads is just as important as what goes on between them in their interpersonal relationships" (Framo, 1981).

Ivan Boszormenyi-Nagy (1973, 1981) is also associated with psychodynamic family therapy. He makes an important point critical to all family therapists—that every family member will internalize the therapist's qualities of empathy and trust-worthiness. Although Whitaker's (1977) highly personal style is often termed existential, much of what he shares with a family is very psychodynamic, particularly his use of fantasies and dreams. He encourages patients to relate their fantasies about family members in order to convert fantasy into workable interpersonal reactions.(For instance, a suicidal client relates fantasies about who the spouse would marry, how long their children would be sad, etc.) He encourages the expression of fantasy alternatives to intrafamilial strife (If you were to kill your husband instead of yourself, how would you do it?). Whitaker (1977) also suggests that the therapist share his or her own dreams with a family to encourage them to discuss dreams in therapy as well as to share them with each other to enhance meaningful communication.

BOWEN'S SYSTEMS FAMILY THERAPY

In Bowen's (1971) approach the cognitive is emphasized and every attempt is made to eliminate the use of affect. Systems theory focuses on triangulation, which implies that whenever there is emotional distance or conflict between two individuals, tensions will be displaced onto a third party, issue, and/or substance. Alcohol and drugs are frequently the subject of triangulation , and so Bowen's approach can be very helpful in understanding substance abusers and helping them to change.

The genogram, another contribution of Bowen, has become a basic tool in many family therapy approaches. A genogram is a pictorial chart of the people involved in a three-generational relationship system; it marks marriages, divorces, births, geographical locations, illnesses, and deaths. All significant physical, social, and psychological dysfunctions may be added to it. The genogram is used to examine relationships in the extended family complex (Guerin & Pendagast, 1976).

Another related helpful diagnostic tool developed by systems theorists is the family chronology, which is a time map of major family events and stresses. The chronology enables the family and therapist to understand the evolution of family patterns over time. The chronology and the genogram "elicit the facts about the structural characteristics, membership, nodal events and toxic issues in a family" (Guerin & Pendagast, 1976). One of the major benefits of this approach is that many important conflicts and stresses that otherwise might not come out until much later are unearthed in the first session or two. The genogram and chronology emphasize another aspect of the systems approach, which is to deemotionalize and objectify data. This is not to deny that strong affect will be released in the early phases of this type of therapy. However, further attempts to achieve insight should be suspended until the initial affect is resolved.   Systems theory emphasizes that family therapy can be done even if only one individual is available. This is done in five phases: engagement, planning, re-entry work, the work, and follow-through (Carter & Orfanides, 1976). Berenson (1984) uses an adaptation of the Bowen's system model viewing the treatment of the alcoholic and his family as progressing in three stages which are related to issues of closeness and distance. In the first phase termed *wet* the family is worked with to achieve an alcohol free state as described in detail in chapter 7. Here, an important goal in addition to achieving an abstinent state is encouraging the cycles of spousal approach/avoidance. This is facilitated by encouraging emotional distance on the part of the family which enables the alcoholic to stop drinking or on the other hand by the behavior confrontation described as an intervention in chapter 7.

Berenson terms the second phase *adaptation* to sobriety. One critical aspect of this phase is that the therapist works to postpone spousal intimacy until the phase is worked through. Since this second stage lasts 6–12 months, Berenson would suggest that many therapists strive for spousal intimacy much too soon after sobriety. This early push to intimacy may explain many therapeutic failures with these families as the threat of intimacy before the alcoholic or family is ready to tolerate it may set off alcoholic drinking patterns. However, many therapeutic maneuvers are necessary to prepare the spouses for intimacy. Thus, Berenson focuses on the alcoholic's relationship to his children, particularly reestablishing the parenting role. In addition, he works on the family of origin of both spouses looking for repetitive intergenerational problems and triangles which lead to alcohol related behaviors. In this phase he also works with the alcoholic to develop ways of having fun without drinking. If the sober spouse complains that she wants more intimacy during this phase, then she is urged to go beyond expressing her anger and hurt feelings in order to deal with her fears of emptiness. If the former alcoholic is undermining or placating, than this is a signal that they are not ready for intimacy and the therapist moves them away from spousal issues. If the latter responds in a supportive manner, then the family is ready to move to stage three *maintenance* or restoration of spousal intimacy. Both adaptation and maintenance proceed slowly and the therapist should be pleased with slow, gradual improvement.

BEHAVIORAL FAMILY THERAPY

This approach is one of the most widely used family therapy approaches with alcoholics and substance abusing adolescents. Its popularity may be attributed to the fact that it can be elaborated in clear, easily learned steps. Noel and McCrady (1983) have outlined these steps as they are applied to specific cases in short-term therapy.

- in the *functional analysis phase*, couples are taught to understand their interactions that maintain drinking, and the alcoholic is taught to quantitate alcohol consumption (three sessions).
- In the *stimulus control phase* (two sessions) the therapist teaches specific techniques to avoid drinking by viewing it "as a habit triggered by certain antecedents and maintained by certain consequences." The client is taught to avoid or change these triggers.
- The third phase is called *rearranging contingencies* (three sessions). Here the client is taught techniques to provide reinforcement for efforts at achieving sobriety: (1) reviewing the positive consequences of sobriety as contrasted to a list of negative consequences, three to four times daily; (2) self-contracting for goals and specific rewards for achieving these goals, and (3) covert reinforcement by rehearsing in fantasy a scene in which the client resists a strong urge to drink (Noel & McCrady, 1983).
- In the *cognitive restructuring phase*, clients are taught to modify self-derogatory, retaliatory, or guilt-related thoughts, which often precipitate drinking. Clients question the logic of these "irrational" thoughts and replace them with more "rational" ideations.
- The fifth phase consists of one session to plan alternatives to drinking. Clients are taught techniques for refusing drinks through role playing and covert reinforcement.
- The sixth phase (two sessions) is used for problem solving and assertion. Here the client is helped to decide if a situation calls for an assertive response and then, through role playing, develops effective assertive techniques. Clients are to perform these techniques twice daily as well as utilize them in a difficult situation which would have previously triggered the urge to drink.
- In the fifteenth and final session, termed *maintenance planning*, the entire course of therapy is reviewed and the new armamentarium of skills is emphasized. Clients are encouraged to practice these skills regularly as well

as re-read handout materials that explain and reinforce these skills.

Even if the reader is not trained in behavioral techniques, these techniques can be extremely helpful in the families of any type of substance abuser.

Stuart (1980) utilizes a variation of behavioral therapy which he terms a social learning approach. He has developed a number of techniques that may be extremely helpful, with couples who have been distanced for years through substance abuse and who are prepared to gradually build closeness. One critical technique is termed "caring days" which is based on the principal of each partner acting "as if" they cared for the other. Each partner is asked what they would like the other to do as a way of showing that they care. A list of behaviors is written in the center of a page and each partner writes the dates on their side of the page that they have performed these behaviors. The therapist helps reframe the behaviors so that they are positive, specific, "small" enough to be performed daily, and not the subject of recent sharp conflict. The couple should be coached to list 18 behaviors and add several new ones weekly. Each should commit to performing at least five behaviors daily and each is expected to change before the other. The "caring days" overcome the couple's fear of change by utilizing small nonconflictual behaviors that are promptly reinforced as building blocks before dealing with more difficult behaviors. Stuart also helps couples become aware of their nonverbal communication in order to make the nonverbal message concordant with the verbal and to learn to express interpersonal warmth nonverbally as well as verbally.

REFERENCES

Ackerman, N.W. Family psychotherapy and psychoanalysis: The implications of difference. In N.W. Ackerman (Ed.), *Family process.* New York: Basic Books, 1970.

Berenson, D. *Treating the alcoholic system after the drinking stops.* Presentation to AFTA, New York, New York, June 18, 1984.

Boszormenyi-Nagy, I., & Spark, G. *Invisible loyalties.* New York: Harper & Row, 1973.

Boszormenyi-Nagy, I., & Ulrich, D.N. Contextual family therapy. In A.S. Gurman & D.P. Kniskern (Eds.), *Handbook of family therapy.* New York: Brunner/Mazel, 1981.

Bowen, M. Family therapy and family group therapy. In H. Kaplan & B. Sadock (Eds.), *Comprehensive group psychotherapy,* New York: Williams & Wilkins, 1971.

Carter, E., & Orfanides, M.N. Family therapy with one person and the family therapist's own family. In P. Guerin (Ed.), *Family therapy.* New York: Gardner Press, 1976, 193–210.

Framo, J.L. The integration of marital therapy with sessions with family of origin. In. A.J. Gurman & D.P. Kniskern (Eds.), *Handbook of family therapy.* New York: Brunner/Mazel, 1981, 133–158.

Framo, J.L. Family of origin as a therapeutic resource for adults in marital and family therapy: You can and should go home again. *Family Process,* 1976, *15,* 193–210.

Guerin, P.J., & Pendagast, E.G. Evaluation of family system and genogram. In P.J. Guerin (Ed.), *Family therapy.* New York: Gardner Press, 1976, 450–464.

Gurman, A.S., & Kniskern, D.P. *Handbook of family therapy.* New York: Brunner/Mazel, 1981.

Haley, L. *Problem solving therapy.* San Francisco: Josey Bass, 1977.

Hoffman, L. The strategic approach and Haley's problem solving approach. In L. Hoffman (Ed.), *Foundations of family therapy.* New York: Basic Books, 1981, 271–283.

Kaufman, E. The application of the basic principles of family therapy to the treatment of drug and alcohol abusers. In Kaufman & Kaufman (Eds.), *Family therapy of drug and alcohol abuse.* New York: Gardner Press, 1979, 255–272.

Mandanes, C. Elements of strategic family therapy, in C. Mandanes (Ed.), *Strategic family therapy.* New York: Josey-Bass, 1981, 19–28.

Minuchin, S. *Families and family therapy.* Cambridge, MA: Harvard University Press, 1974.

Noel, N.E., & McCrady, B.S. Behavioral treatment of an alcohol abuser with the spouse present, in Kaufman, E. (Ed.), *Power to change: Family case studies in the treatment of alcoholism.* New York: Gardner, 1984.

Papp, P. The Greek chorus and other techniques of paradoxical therapy. *Family Process,* 1980, *19,* 45–58.

Palazolli-Selvini, M., Boscolo, L., Cecchin, G., & Prata, G. Hypothesizing-circularity-neutrality three guidelines for the conductor of the session. *Family Process*, 1980, *19*, 3–12.

Skynner, A.C.R. An open systems, group analytic approach to family therapy, in Gurman, A. & Kniskern, D. (Eds.), *Book of family therapy*. New York: Brunner-Mazel, 1981, 39–84.

Skynner, A.C.R. *Systems of family and marital psychotherapy*. New York: Brunner/Mazel, 1976.

Stanton, M.D. An integrated structural/strategic approach to family therapy. *Journal of marital and family therapy, 1981, 7*, 427–439.

Stuart, R.B. *Helping couples change*. New York: Guilford, 1980.

Whitaker, C. Process techniques of family therapy. *Interaction.* 1977, *1*, 4–19.

Chapter 9

Structural–Dynamic Family Therapy Techniques with Substance Abusers—A Personal Synthesis

In the preceding chapter, I summarized many schools of family therapy that are of substantial value in the treatment of substance abusers especially the work of Minuchin and Haley. Their influence has been so great that readers familiar with their writings will be aware that many of their family therapy techniques have been adapted to apply to my work with substance abusers. My approach also borrows from systems and psychoanalytic techniques and integrates these disparate treatment methods into one system. The reader is advised to choose those methods that are compatible with his or her personality, to first learn and practice these techniques by rote, and finally to utilize them in a spontaneous manner. These techniques will be described individually, although most techniques incorporate several others as they are implemented. As a complement to this chapter on techniques, Chapter 11 presents several case histories and dicusses the relevant treatment methods.

FAMILY DIAGNOSIS

Diagnosis is a cornerstone of my family approach. In family diagnosis, we do not pin a DSM III label on every individual member. Rather we look at family interactional and communication patterns and relationships. I prefer a family systems approach that utilizes structural concepts (described in Chapter 8) but also considers a psychodynamic understanding of the personality of each individual. However, unlike most psychoanalytic approaches, the therapist is urged to become a part of the family and actively to shift his or her own alliances within the family system. In addition, diagnosis is made in a flexible way, with the diagnostic structural family map changing every session (Kaufman 1979). Using the structural model, I examine the family's rules, roles, boundaries, and flexibilities. I look for coalitions, particularly transgenerational ones, shifting alliances, splits, cutoffs, and triangulation. I observe communication patterns, confirmation and disconfirmation, unclear messages, and conflict resolution. I note the family's stage in the family life cycle. I note mind reading (predicting reactions and reacting to them before they happen, or knowing what someone thinks or wants), double binds, and fighting styles. In the first visit, I rarely use an extended genogram (which includes all aunts, uncles and cousins), but I always obtain an abbreviated, three-generational genogram that focuses on the identified patient (IP), his or her parents and progeny, and the spouses's parents. In addition, I include other members of the household and any other significant relatives with whom there is regular or important current contact. In step-families, the initial genogram must include the noncustodial parent(s) and the geographical location and family situation of all children from prior marriages, as these may be extremely significant. As therapy progresses, a full but informal family genogram is gradually developed as other important family members from the past and present are discussed. The genogram provides a cast of significant characters in the family so that a diagnostic map may be constructed.

The most common family systems are mapped as follows:

- Male adolescent substance abuser triangulated by conflictual parents and enmeshed with mother (M = mother, F = father, C = child):

- Dependent alcoholic father with male parental child and overinvolved spouse. Father is overinvolved with daughter.

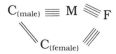

These family maps focus on the need to shift coalitions in these families and restore appropriate parental heirarchy. Once the therapist has mastered the concept of family maps, it is not necessary to formulate them on paper as they become automatically imaged and shifted in the therapist's mind's eye. Other aspects of family diagnosis may be borrowed from other family therapy systems.

In assessing a family and its members, it is critical to assess their strengths as well as weaknesses.

THE CONTRACT

The contract is an agreement to work on mutually agreed upon, workable issues. The contract should always promise help with the IP's problems before it is expanded to other issues. Goals should be mutual. If there is disagreement about them, then work on resolving disagreements should be made a part of the contract.

The preliminary contract is drafted with the family at the end of the first interview. In subsequent sessions, the concept of a contract is always maintained so that family assignments and tasks are agreed upon and their implementation contracted by the family. When an individual or agency chooses an initial assessment period of more than one session, then the contract at the end of the first session may include only an agreement by the family to participate in the planned evaluation. However, the likelihood that the family will return after the first session is greatly enhanced by a contract that develops measures for problem resolution. All initial contracts include the length of therapy, duration of sessions, cost, and which members will attend and in what combinations. The therapist may also choose to include his or her style, techniques, and expectations of the family. Everyone in the household and all other involved family members such as grandparents and siblings away at college should be invited and urged to attend sessions. The greater the number of family members involved, the more thoroughly the family is understood. When working with a family system that appears limited to the mother–addict diad, it is particularly important to involve a third member to provide sufficient leverage for structural change.

The length of therapy may be flexibly renegotiated at the end of the initial time period, particularly if family members feel they have made noticeable gains. Whereas the initial contract should provide for some relief of the symptoms of the identified patient, subsequent contracts, if agreed to, can focus on other family members. There are many specific modifications of the contract with substance abusers. The family must choose a system to achieve abstinence and agree to pursue that system after it has been agreed upon as part of the initial evaluation (see Chapter 7 for examples of systems to achieve abstinence). In addition, family members other than the IP must agree to a type of support group and to the location and number of meetings they will attend. Involving all siblings and both parents in treatment is an important aspect of the contract. In order to do this it is essential that the therapist be sufficiently flexible to be available at times when all family members can be present or to make home visits when necessary.

The family should be provided with the beginnings of a system of shifting overreactivity to substance abuse in the initial contract. They may be coached to disengage from the IP, using strength gained from support groups and the therapist. At times, this disengagement can only be accomplished by powerful restructuring or paradoxical interventions. Later in therapy, contingency contracting principles can be used to facilitate mutual trust, particularly in areas such as adolescent individuation (e.g., a child agrees to be more respectful if curfew is extended).

JOINING

In joining, the therapist adjusts himself or herself in a number of different ways in order to affiliate with the family system. Joining enhances the therapist's leverage to change the system. The therapist alternates between joining that supports the family system and its members and joining that challenges it. Joining with only one part of a family may severely stress and/or change the rest of the family.

In joining with the family, the therapist alternates between existential engagement and disengaged expertise. The therapist must be capable of joining each subsystem, including that of siblings. Each family member must be able to feel the therapist's respect for him or her as an individual as well as the therapist's firm commitment to healing. The therapist must make contact with all family members so that they will comply with the therapist even when they sense that he or she is being unfair (Kaufman, 1979). With the families of substance abusers, the therapist must join with them by respecting and not challenging their initial defensiveness.

Joining begins when the family first enters the office. I begin the first session by a series of contacts with each member. I shake everyone's hand, take pains to remember each person's name, and introduce myself as Dr. Ed Kaufman to each member. The family is immediately put at ease by this contact, which is followed by a brief chat, consisting of small talk, with each member. Minuchin has categorized joining by two different systems, techniques (1974) and proximity (1981).

Techniques of Joining

There are three types of joining techniques: maintenance, tracking, and mimesis.

Maintenance

Maintenance requires supporting the family structures and behaving according to the family rules. The therapist may initially speak to the family through the family spokesperson or "switchboard." When a family is being pushed beyond its ability to tolerate stress, maintenance techniques can be used to lower stress. Maintenance operations include supporting areas of family strength, rewarding, affiliating with a family member, complimenting/supporting a threatened member, and explaining a problem. The therapist uses the family's metaphors, expressions, and language. For example, an alcoholic husband and his wife fought over every issue endlessly and repetitively. Since they played chess, they were instructed to declare a "stalemate" whenever they repeated an argument three times and thus end the argument. This is also an example of using a code word to end an argument by helping a family to laugh at themselves and their repeated angry cycles.

Al-Anon members use the phrase "release with love" to help them disengage from a substance-abusing child or spouse. In substance-abusing families there is often more than one substance abuser but until the family has identified them as such, it is important to not deal with them. At times substance abuse by others may be dealt with subtly if it is in the context of the problems of the IP, such as asking a father to not drink at dinner so that he and his spouse can set limits on an acting-out adolescent. Thus, the therapist enters the family as a supporter of family rules but makes the rules work in the direction of therapeutic goals for the family.

Joining with every member of the family is part of the art of therapy. The family therapist does not have to be tattooed and speak in four-letter words in order to relate to an adolescent drug abuser, but a thorough knowledge of and tolerance for the vernacular is essential. With older alcoholics, a certain respect for the pristine language of sobriety as well as a basic knowledge of the 12 steps of Alcoholics Anonymous is likewise important.

Tracking

In tracking, the therapist follows the content of the family's interactions by listening carefully to what everyone has to say and by providing comments and expressions that help each family member know he or she has been heard and understood.

Mimesis

Mimesis involves the therapist's adopting the family's style and affect as reflected by the members' action and needs. If a family uses humor, so should the therapist, but without double binds. If a family communicates through touching, then the therapist should also touch. The therapist might join an isolated father by sharing pipe utensils or a cigarette, or join a frightened member by moving his or her chair next to that person.

In one family I worked with there was an isolated father who was distant from everyone, including the therapeutic team. The only thing I could find in common with him was that we both had moustaches, though his was carefully waxed. Not conscious of the act being related to him, I found myself purchasing moustache wax for the first time in years and applying it before my session with him. I find that this helped me to join with him. However, I am best able to identify with most disengaged family members by understanding them, helping them change, or identifiying latent or overt common aspects of personality.

Mimesis is frequently done unconsciously and is readily used in family systems therapy, in contrast to individual psychoanalytic psychotherapy, where it is generally contraindicated, as are most overt joining techniques. Sharing food in sessions or in multiple-family therapy encourages a joining of all members present as well as uniting the therapist with each member. Ultimately, the most significant joining occurs when the therapist communicates to the family that he or she understands them and is working with and for them. Thus, paradoxically, the most profound joining comes when the therapist challenges the family's dysfunctional maneuvers which gives them hope that the therapist can make them better.

Joining with all family members may be too difficult for one therapist, particularly in families with an adolescent IP. I have often found it necessary to utilize a co-therapist who treats the adolescent advocate postion in the family sessions. This enables me to better join with parents and facilitate their limit setting. In other cases, the adolescent is begging for limits underneath their bravado and a single therapist can easily join with the adolescent as well as the parental system.

Joining Classified by Proximity

In joining families from a close proximity the therapist must push him or herself to find positive aspects in all family members, particularly ones who are disliked (Minuchin & Fishman,

1981). A therapist who finds something positive in someone unlikeable will find that he or she then begins to like them. Another technique is for the therapist to look into his or her own personality and find similar (but less exaggerated) characteristics. By confirming these positives the therapist will enhance the individual's self-esteem and help make that person more likeable. In general, pointing out several individuals' complimentary responsiblility for negative behaviors will help the therapist to join with the entire system. In joining from a middle position the therapist gathers important information by observing his or her own ways of interacting with the family without being incorporated into the family system. Here it is often important to shift emphasis by tracking from content to process. In joining from a disengaged position, the therapist may have the role of an expert or director. Families who come to a therapist or institution that has an outstanding reputation will readily comply with tasks and other directives. Perhaps even more than most techniques, joining becomes much more spontaneous and less deliberate as therapy progresses.

RESTRUCTURING

Unlike joining, restructuring involves a challenge to the family's homeostasis and takes place through changing the family affiliations and interactional patterns. In restructuring, the therapist uses expertise in social manipulation, with the word "manipulation" being used in a positive, rather than a perjorative sense. Techniques used for change include actualization, marking boundaries, assigning tasks, reframing, paradox, balancing and unbalancing, creating intensity, and psychodynamic techniques. Joining is necessary as a prerequisite and facilitator for change production, and the therapist frequently alternates between joining and restructuring.

Probing refers to the concept of evaluating the system's ability to change by its response to therapeutic maneuvers. It is not a specific therapeutic technique, although every therapeutic intervention is a probe. Probing permits the therapist a wide spectrum of interventions while observing how the family system responds. Resistence to the probe reveals rigidity, and compliance demonstrates resilience. A rebuffed probe leads to retreat and perhaps joining. A successful probe opens the way for further interventions. Probes may lead directly to learning and change by the family, activate alternatives, or unbalance homeostasis, which then results in longterm changes. As the family responds to probing, the family diagnosis is reevaluated and reflected in shifts in "the map."

Actualizing Family Transactional Patterns

Patients usually direct their communications to the therapist. They should be trained to talk to each other rather than to the therapist. They should be asked to enact transactional patterns rather than describe them. Role playing and family sculpting (having a family member position everyone in a characteristic posture) are helpful ways to facilitate actualization of patterns as well as change them. Manipulating space is a powerful tool for generating actualization. Changing seating may create or strengthen boundaries. Asking two members who have been chronically disengaged and/or communicating through a third party to sit next to each other can actualize strong conflicts and emotions.

Alcoholic families frequently gravitate to a rehash of past fights, hoping to entrap the therapist into deciding who started the fight, who is wrong and right, and what the proper decision is. It is critical not to be triangulated into such a position but rather to have the family choose an as yet unresolved conflict and actualize their problem-solving methods or lack of them in the session. If a family arrives with an intoxicated member they should not be dismissed but their interactions observed, as this will demonstrate how they interact during a good proportion of their time together. Of course, if intoxication is a repeated problem then the family must develop a system to end the substance abuse (see Chapter 7).

Most families will enter therapy trying to look as good as possible. Actualizations unleash sequences which are beyond their control and permit the therapist to see the family as it really is. Three progressively elaborated types of actualization are utilized (Minuchin & Fishman, 1981). The first involves sequences which evolve spontaneously as families are permitted to be themselves in session. Next, the therapist plans scenarios that permit further natural interactions. These may utilize latent issues that are close to the surface and are beginning to evolve in session. In the most change-oriented types of actualization, the therapist has the family re-enact in the session a pattern that is outside of their repetitive, maladaptive system and demonstrates new ways of problem solving.

Marking Boundaries

A basic rule of thumb, which may even be a part of the therapeutic contract, is preservation of individual boundaries. That is, each person should be spoken *to*, not *about*, and no one should talk, feel, think, answer, or act for anyone else. Each family member is encouraged to tell his or her own story, and should listen to and acknowledge the communications of others. Nonverbal checking and blocking of communications should also be observed and when appropriate, pointed out and halted. "Mind reading" is very common but is strongly discouraged because even if the mind reader is correct it almost always starts an argument. No one likes his or her reactions to be anticipated.

Symbolic boundaries are established in the session by the therapist placing his or her body, an arm, or a piece of furniture between members, by rearranging members, or by avoiding eye contact. These boundaries are supported and strengthened by tasks outside of the session. The most important boundary shift is weakening the ties between an overinvolved parent and child and strengthening the boundary that protects them from inlaws, affairs, and the rest of the world external to the nuclear family.

If a role or tie is removed from a family member, this relationship should be replaced by building ties with other family members or people outside of the family. At times a dominating family figure may be asked to not attend for a few sessions or to watch a session through a one-way mirror and comment later on the process. Al-Anon and Alateen may also be used to reinforce individual boundaries.

Children should not be lumped together as substance abusers or "bad" and "good" kids. They should be differentiated and given rights and privileges according to their ages and position in the family. Likewise, adult substance abusers should not be assumed to be identical. The power of parents may also be differentiated but must be perfectly clear to each spouse, particularly in step-families. Hospitalization may often be necessary with substance abusers and its boundary-marking powers should not be neglected.

In general, when boundaries around a system are strengthened, that system functions better (unless, of course, boundaries are dysfunctionally disengaged prior to intervention).

Assigning Tasks

Tasks are perhaps the most important technique in family therapy, representing the major road to change in much the same way transference does in individual psychoanalytic psychotherapy. There are three major purposes of tasks (Haley, 1977):

1. to gather information through tasks that probe and actualize.
2. to intensify the relationship with the therapist and to continue the therapeutic change process outside of the session.
3. to enable people to behave differently.

There are many *ways to motivate families to perform tasks,* some of which flow from other aspects of the principles of family therapy (Haley, 1977):

1. Join the family first, using family language and metaphors to frame the tasks.
2. Chose tasks in the framework of family goals, particularly those that are directed towards correcting the symptoms of the IP.
3. Choose tasks that bring gains to each member of the family, particularly if there is conflict about doing the tasks.
4. Ask what solutions have been tried and failed in order to enhance therapeutic leverage.

5. Ask what has worked in the past and why it was abandoned, as it may work again.
6. Accept the family's desperation, as it will motivate them to follow the tasks.
7. Have the family accomplish a task in session before they are given one for homework.
8. If family members are improving, use their progress to prescribe further change so they can improve even more.
9. Use your position as an expert to emphasize the need to perform the tasks.
10. Cut off disagreement about doing the tasks and tell them to "do it anyway."
11. Provide the general framework of the tasks and let the family work with you to develop the specifics.

Haley (1977) has also made a number of suggestions for *how to properly give tasks* so that they will be successfully accomplished. I have also integrated these into my work as rules of thumb with substance-abusing families:

1. Be specific.
2. Give the tasks clearly, concisely, and firmly.
3. Formulate the tasks throughout the session, highlighting important areas, but be certain to emphasize all specific tasks at the end of the session.
4. Be as repetitious as necessary to have the family remember the tasks. Have each family member repeat and/or write down the tasks and his or her role.
5. Involve everyone in the household. One person may perform the task, another help, and another supervise, plan, or check on it.
6. Review how each family member may avoid performing his or her role or prevent completion of the task.
7. Make the task part of contracting at the end of each session.
8. Remember the task, writing it down specifically if this is necessary for full recall.
9. Review the task at the beginning of the next session.

10. Use failures as learning experiences to reveal the dysfunctional aspects of the family or the poor timing of the task. Support the family in what they have learned from not doing the task.
11. Remember that negotiations about the task may be more important than the actual task.
12. Do not let the family off easily, particularly if they forget the task. Explore why they let themselves down.
13. Build incrementally from easy to more difficult tasks.
14. Tasks should be used to achieve structural change.
15. Always assign at least one task per session.
16. Avoid assigning more than two or three tasks in a session.

The tasks should always be compatible with the therapist's goals for restructuring the family. Therapeutic homework assignments permit the therapists and the therapeutic work to live with the family until the next session (Kaufman & Pattison, 1981).

As examples of specific tasks, a couple might be asked to speak to each other in the session while facing each other directly and without a child sitting between them. If this is successful, then they can be assigned to eat dinner in a restaurant without their children, or to take a vacation by themselves. To build closeness, a couple can be given the task of planning a pleasant surprise for each other and not revealing what it is until the following session. This may put each member in a frame of mind where they are constantly thinking of what they can do for the other. One couple that had recently separated took this task to heart. The husband brought a new set of wedding bands and his wife arranged for a remarriage in a church. (However, it is important to note that this type of task can also cause a great deal of anger and distancing in families where there is an inability to give or receive, as anger is heightened by unsuccessful closeness-building tasks.)

A husband was asked to plan a sexual surprise for his wife in return for her surprise of the previous week. When this was successful, they were asked to share their sexual fantasies with each other and chose one to act out. A father who had neglected his medical and dental care because he was worried about his wife's drinking was asked to make an appointment with a dentist. A wife who was overinvolved with the amount of alcohol her husband was consuming daily was given the task of estimating how many drinks he had every day and writing it down without telling him. He was asked to write down the actual amounts, and they were compared in the next session. The discrepancies demonstrated the futility of her efforts to control him and diminished her overinvolvement in his drinking. This task was also a paradoxical one (see "Paradox" below). More detailed examples of how tasks are utilized over the course of treatment will be given in Chapters 10 & 11.

Reframing

In reframing (Minuchin & Fishman, 1981), the therapist takes information received from the family and transforms it into a format that will be most helpful to changing the family. Reframing begins at the start of the first session as the therapist receives information from the family, molding it so that the family feels that their problems are clear and solvable. Reframing is achieved by focusing material as it is received, selecting the elements that will facilitate change and organizing the information in such a way as to give it new meaning. Perhaps the most common use of reframing is when the symptoms of an identified patient are broadened to include the entire family system. (As an example, from the symptom of John, the child in a family, taking drugs, the therapist might reframe as, John takes drugs because he feels it will keep his parents together, and the parents need John to use drugs because dealing with his crises keeps them from looking at emptiness in their own relationship.)

Behavior may be reframed in order to broaden its focus—from the IP to the family, from problems at school to problems in the home, from substance abuse to intrafamilial abuse. Problems and failures can be reframed as learning experiences. Reframing is also frequently used to shift behavior to a more positive light or "normalize" it. Thus adolescent rebelliousness that is overreacted to by parents can be labeled as "normal individuation." A couple's constant battling can be reframed as their intense need for each other's love. A couple who repeatedly and intensely put each other down might be told that each is trying to prove to the world that the spouse is an inept "jerk," and to think about what that says about themselves.

The Paradox

As the meaning and uses of the paradox have been described in detail under strategic therapy in Chapter 8, I will focus here on how paradox is integrated into my personal therapeutic system. I prefer to use in general a more directive, structural approach, shifting to paradox mainly when the structural approach is not successful. I find that paradoxical techniques work best with chronicly rigid, repetitive, circular, highly resistant family systems, particularly ones that have had many prior therapeutic failures (Papp, 1981). In certain situations that seem to call for a paradoxical intervention I find difficulty using this technique, perhaps because it feels dishonest to me, but in other situations application of a paradox feels much more comfortable and natural.

I will not use paradox when family motivation is high, resistance is low, and the family responds readily to direct interventions (Papp, 1981). I do not use paradox in crisis situations such as violence, suicide, incest, or child abuse; here the therapist needs to provide structure and control. I avoid paradox with paranoid IPs and in families with widespread mistrust. I *will* use paradox to slow progress so that a family is chafing at the bit to move faster, or I may exaggerate a symptom to emphasize the family's need to extrude it. An example of this is encouraging a family to continue the "glories" of overindulging and infantilizing a substance abuser. A symptom that is an externalized acting-out of family conflicts (stealing, secret drinking) can be prescribed to be performed within the family so that the family can deal with it. I do not prescribe an individual's behavior without relating it to its function in the family system. The symptom should *only* be prescribed if its function in the system is understood and if it can be prescribed in a way which changes the functioning of the system. At times it seems to me that paradox is a way of making a psychodynamic or system interpretation which motivates the family to change behavior in a way that classical interpretations do not e.g. encouraging an adolescent to continue to act out because his parents need the behavior to argue about in order to avoid feeling close enough to have a sexual relationship.

The beginning therapist should avoid several pitfalls in applying paradoxical techniques:

1. Being too pat and not tailoring the intervention to meet a family's specific needs.
2. Being too mechanistic and distant and/or overlooking affective cues so that the family feels misunderstood.
3. Using paradox to deal with your own frustration with the family's lack of change.
4. Not relating the directive to the behavior's function in the family system.
5. Giving up when the family doesn't respond immediately.
6. Undoing the paradoxical thrust by supporting initial changes with a great degree of enthusiasm.
7. Relying exclusively on paradox when direct restructuring is indicated.
8. Being disappointed with your therapeutic efforts merely because you are not working paradoxically.

Balancing and Unbalancing

The therapist moves back and forth between balancing and unbalancing. Balancing techniques tend to support a family and unbalancing to stress the family system.

Balancing is similar to Minuchin and Fishman's *complementarity* (1981). It challenges the family's views of symptoms as part of a linear hierarchy and emphasizes the reciprocal involvement of symptom formation, while supporting the family. Mutual responsibility should be emphasized and tasks that involve change in all parties should be given. The therapist must be aware that an individual's view of his or her responsibility for a symptom may be so skewed that what the therapist feels is perfectly balanced may feel very unbalanced and unfair to that person.

Unbalancing involves changing or stressing the existing hierarchy in a family and should only be attempted after the therapist has achieved a great deal of power through joining. The therapist unbalances by affiliating with a family member of low power so this person can challenge his or her prescribed family role, or by escalating a crisis: emphasizing differences, blocking typical transactional patterns, developing implicit conflict, and rearranging the hierarchy (Minuchin & Fishman, 1981). The therapist may also paradoxically unbalance by affiliating with a dominant member in order to elicit a challenging response from those of less power. What is critical here is that the therapist's affiliation unbalances and interrupts rigid, repetitive cycles. The therapist may alternate affiliations so that the family explores new ways of relating rather than competing for position. When a therapist joins in alliance or coalition with a family member or subsystem, it is critical that it be for restructuring purposes rather than for the likes and dislikes of the therapist. It is also critical that the therapist be able to extricate him-or herself as necessary. If support of one member is intolerable for the family, then the therapist may have to retreat to a more balanced approach. Unbalancing may be difficult for some therapists because it feels "unfair."

Creating Intensity

These techniques (Minuchin & Fishman, 1981) enable the family to hear and incorporate the messages sent by the therapist. One simple way to be heard is to repeat either the same phrase or different phrases that convey the same concept. Another way of creating intensity, isomorphic transaction, uses isomorphic transactions which are many interventions to attack the same underlying dysfunctional pattern. The amount of time a family spends on a transaction can be increased or decreased, as can the proximity of members during an interaction. Intensity can also be created by resisting the family's pull to get the therapist to do what they want. Creating intensity should not be confused with escalating a crisis, which was described above and is based on severe unbalancing rather than on being heard (Minuchin & Fishman, 1981).

PSYCHODYNAMIC CONCEPTS AND TECHNIQUES

Psychodynamic techniques are those that utilize the past to change the present; they focus on unconscious thought process. The symptoms of the IP are viewed in the context of his/her own historical past as well as that of every family member. Psychodynamic family therapy and strategic therapies have a common ultimate goal: achieving second-order change. The goal is to change the entire family system so that dysfunction does not occur in other family members once the symptoms of the IP have been alleviated.

Psychodynamic techniques can be very useful if they are applied to the present in a here and now way. The past is explored only to change the future. The past is not dwelled on to rationalize behavior or to replay old patterns of guilt induction and hostility. Some families, who live the present through past events and feelings, can only deal with the present after they have expunged their past hurts.

There are two cornerstones for the implementation of psychodynamic techniques: the therapist's self-knowledge and a detailed family history. Every family member will internalize a therapist's good qualities, such as warmth, trust, trustworthiness, assertion, empathy, and understanding. Likewise, they may incorporate less-desirable qualities such as anger, despair, and emotional distancing. It is absolutely essential that a therapist thoroughly understand his or her own emotional reactions as well as their relationship to the therapist's family of origin and nuclear family. This self-knowledge can be obtained by some combination of intensive individual therapy, family therapy, and family of origin work. The lack of such knowledge will repeatedly interfere with the therapist's work with families. Some of these problems can be corrected by their being pointed out repeatedly, particularly in live supervision, but others cannot be shifted without psychotherapy or F of O work. (Live supervision means that a therapist's work is viewed through a one-way mirror and instructions called in during the session or during a break.)

The more a therapist understands about a family's history and prior patterns, the better he/she will be able to help that family to not repeat dysfunctional transactions or personalized transference reactions. When a couple is stuck, I will frequently use individual sessions for both partners which focus on their own family of origin in an attempt to understand and shift patterns which are being repeated unchanged over several generations.

The psychodynamic concepts discussed will be countertransference, interpretation, resistance and working through.

The Use of Countertransference

Many therapists are unable to utilize supervisory suggestions even during live supervision. A major reason for this is countertransference. The therapist's uncontrolled emotional reactions may be to either the content or the accompanying affect of an issue being discussed. The therapist may feel great power from being a therapist and feel disdain for patients and their "lower status." The therapist may have a countertransference problem towards the entire family or any individual member of the family and may get into power struggles. These are, of course, always to be avoided, and they can be if therapists understands their countertransference.

There are specific types of emotional reactions to substance abusers and their families. The IP's dependency, relationship suction and repulsion, manipulativeness, denial, impulsivity, and role abandonment may provoke countertransference reactions in the therapist. However, family therapists view their emotional reactions to families in a systems framework as well as a countertransference context. Thus, they must be aware of how families will replay their problems in therapy by attempting to detour or triangulate their problems onto the therapist. The therapist must be particularly sensitive about becoming a co-alcoholic, who tries to protect or is provoked to reject the alcoholic. The relationship between the therapist and the family replicates what happens within the family at home. One example of this is the therapist who alternates between saving and persecution, first allowing the alcoholic to do almost anything, even coming drunk to sessions, and then switching to a punitive position, for instance, demanding sobriety before therapy can take place. In addition, countertransference must be distinguished from more generalized negativism or hostility toward substance abusers. Both are antitherapeutic. A great deal can be learned about a family from tuning into countertransference.

Judicious expression of these feelings may at times be helpful in breaking fixed family patterns. For example, sharing anger at a controlling parent may give the family enough support to do so in a manner that is acceptable to that person.

The Role of Interpretation

Interpretations can be extremely helpful if they are made in a complimentary way, without blaming, guilt induction, or dwelling on the hopelessness of longstanding, fixed patterns. Repetitive patterns and their maladaptive aspects to each family member can be pointed out, and tasks can be given to help them change these patterns. Some families need interpretations before they can fulfill tasks. An emphasis on mutual responsibility when making any interpretation is an example of the helpful fusion of structural and psychodynamic therapy.

Overcoming Resistance

Resistance is defined as behaviors, feelings, patterns, or styles that prevent involvement in therapy or that delay or prevent change (Anderson & Stewart, 1983). In substance-abusing families, key resistance behaviors that must be dealt with involve the failure to perform functions that enable the abuser to stay "clean." It is important to understand resistances and have methods to overcome them. The greater the resistance by the family, the greater the demand on the therapist's energy and creativity. Resistance may be conscious or unconscious, purposeful or accidental, emanate from one family member or from the entire system (Anderson & Stewart, 1983).

Some resistances, such as denial, rationalization, somatization, intellectualization, displacement, and acting out, occur in all types of therapy. Other resistances—collusions, myths, family secrets, scapegoat maintenance, pseudomutuality, and pseudohostility—are specific to family therapy (Anderson & Stewart, 1983).

Every family has characteristic patterns of resistant behavior in addition to isolated resistances. This family "style" may contribute significantly to resistance; some families may need to deny all conflict and emotion and be almost totally unable to tolerate any displays of anger or sadness, while others may overreact to the slightest disagreement. It is important to recognize, emphasize, and interpret the circumstances that arouse resistance patterns (Anderson & Stewart, 1983). However, the therapist must avoid labeling the behavior as "resistance" or directly confronting it, as this increases hostility and in turn enhances resistance. Rather the reciprocal family interactions that lead to resistant behaviors should be pointed out. Anderson and Stewart's recent book, *Mastering Resistance* (1983), contains many excellent methods for dealing with specific resistances. Three general techniques that are widely applicable are asking the family to "try it for just one week," using the extended family and social network, and "shaking things up" or making any change that will challenge the status quo.

Resistance can be focused on in the treatment contract: each family member agrees to cooperate in overcoming resistance. If a family is willing to perform its assigned tasks, then most resistances are irrelevant and/or can be overcome. Resistances such as blaming, dwelling on past injustices, and scapegoating can be directly forbidden by the therapist. The therapist may overcome resistance by joining techniques, including minimizing demands on the family to change so that the family moves more slowly but in the desired direction.

In psychodynamic psychotherapy, the concept of resistance is directly related to change; that is, analysis of resistance is integral and essential to the overall change process. In family therapy, resistance is more often viewed as an obstacle to be overcome. Nevertheless, overcoming family resistance in and of itself may lead to a great deal of positive family change.

Working Through

This important concept, derived from psychoanalysis, is quite similar to the structural concept of isomorphic transactions. It underscores the need to work for an extended time on many different overt issues, all of which stem from the same dsyfunctional core. Thus, in order to have real change, a family must deal with a problem over and over until it has been worked through. In analysis this is termed "the transition from intellectual to genuine or emotional insight." This process is much quicker in family than individual therapy because when an appropriate intervention is made, the entire family system may reinforce the consequent positive change. If the system later pulls the family's behavior back to old maladaptive ways, then it becomes necessary to work the conflicts through in many different transactions until stable change takes place.

One critical type of working through that is often neglected in family therapy is termination. Each individual member should be encouraged to share feelings of loss and, after longterm therapy, grief about giving up therapy and the therapist. No matter how skillfully the therapist attributes the family's gains to the family, they will experience loss. Some families will show their readiness to part by referring another family for treatment; on the other hand, some families reject the therapist's value system as a way of expressing their need to terminate (Whitaker, 1977). Sometimes it is very helpful for the therapist to share his or her own grief as a way of tapping these feelings in the family.

VARIATIONS IN FAMILY THERAPY
TECHNIQUES

Reactivity

In Chapter 2, four family types were presented based on reactivity to alcohol and the alcoholic: functional, enmeshed, disentegrated, and absent. These family types are applicable to drug abuse as well. Family therapy techniques should be modified according to the type and extent of family reactivity.

Functional Families

Functional families have minimal overt conflict and a limited capacity for insight, as they protect their working homeostasis. Thus, the therapist should not be too ambitious to crack the defensive structure of the family, which is likely to be resistant. The initial use of family education is often well received. Explanation of the medical effects of alcoholism and drugs provides a concrete way for the family to face up to the consequences of substance abuse (Kaufman & Pattison, 1981). These families can usually be taught appropriate family rules and roles. Cognitive modes of interaction are usually acceptable, as more uncovering and emotional interactions may be resisted. The exploration of family responses to the substance abuser will uncover dysfunctional behavior that can be modified behaviorally. In general, short-term family therapy aimed at rule definition and role restructing may be sufficient.

If abstinence and equilibrium, are achieved, the therapist should be content even if the family continues to use a great deal of denial and emotional isolation.

The achievement of a "dry system" is usually feasible. Short-term hospitalization may be required. Drug abusers from functional families are often resistant to longterm residential treatment because they are protected by the family homeostasis. This type of alcoholic is often a good candidate for disulfiram (Antabuse) therapy because alcohol can be given up readily without changing or stressing the family. Although it is usually best for the patient or a non-family member to assume responsiblility for administration of Antabuse, the low overt conflict level in these families may permit the non-alcoholic spouse to give it.

Enmeshed Families

The therapeutic approach with enmeshed families is much more difficult and prolonged than with functional families. Educational and behavioral methods may provide some initial relief but are not likely to have much impact on the enmeshed neurotic relationships. Often these families are resistant to ending substance abuse, and the therapist is often faced with working with a wet system until either a dry system is established or the substance abuser is separated from the family.

Although initial hospitalization or detoxification may achieve temporary abstinence, the IP is highly vulnerable to relapse. Therefore long-term family therapy with substantial restructuring is required to develop a non-neurotic family system free of substance abuse. An integrated syntheses of several schools of family therapy techniques may be required.

Because of the enmeshment and explosiveness of these families, it is usually necessary to reinforce boundaries, define personal roles, and diminish reactivity. The therapist will have to be active and directive in order to keep the emotional tensions within workable limits. Disengagement and unmeshing can be assisted by getting family members involved with external support groups such as AA, Al-Anon, Alateen, and N.A. If Anatabuse (disulfiram) is used, the family should not be involved in enforcing its administration, as they will struggle over this in the same way as they did over substance abuse. Methadone maintenance may cool the family down to a point where restructuring can take place.

Disintegrated Family

In disintegrated systems, there is a prior history of reasonable vocational function and family life but a progressive deterioration of family function and, finally, separation from the family. The use of family intervention might seem irrelevant in such a case. However, many of these marriages and families have fallen apart only after severe alcoholism or drug-related behavior. Further, there is often only pseudoindividuation of the substance abuser from marital, family, and kinship ties. There families cannot and will not reconstitute during the early phases of rehabilitation. Early therapeutic sessions are usually characterized by apathy or by intense hostility and denigration of the IP. Thus, the early stages of treatment should focus primarily on the substance abuser. However, potential ties to spouse, family, kin, and friends should be explored early in treatment, and some contact should be initiated. When abstinence and personal stability have been achieved over several months, the family can be worked with to re-establish family ties, but reconstitution of the family unit should not be a necessary goal. It is important that the new roles and relationships be negotiated on the basis of the IP as a recovering alcoholic or exabuser. Some families may not desire a reunion but can achieve healthy separation through short-term family therapy. When reconstitution is not achieved, it is important to negotiate acceptable roles that leave all parties with reasonable self-respect and respect for each other. Otherwise, the IP is likely to be victimized by continuing conflict with the separated family (Kaufman & Pattison, 1981). Should family reconcilation occur, it is desirable to continue family sessions to monitor and stablize new family roles.

Absent Family

In absent family systems there is a totai loss of the family of origin and a lack of other permanent relationships. Nevertheless, there are two types of network interventions possible. The first is the elaboration of still-existing friend and kin contacts. Often these social relationships can be revitalized and provide meaningful social support. Second, in occasional younger patients there is a positive response to peer group approaches, such as longterm therapeutic communities, AA, NA, church fellowships, and recreational and avocational clubs, which draw them into social relationships and vocational rehabilitation. These patients can develop positive new skills and the ability to engage in satisfactory marriage and family life.

Ethnicity

In order to adapt to different ethnic groups, the therapist must first understand the uniqueness of each group. Generally, this knowledge can only be gained by living and/or working with an ethnic group over time. To the extent that these characteristics can be learned from a book, *Ethnicity and Family Therapy* (McGoldrick, Gordano, & Pearce, 1982,) supplies a description of each ethnic group. Four ethnic family types will be described briefly in terms of their specific needs for family ther-

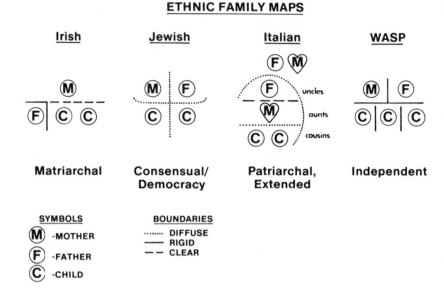

Fig. 9-1. This figure is based on a graph designed with Linda Borders, M.S.W. It appeared in modified form in Adolescent Substance Abuse in Anglo-American Families. *Journal of Drug Issues*, 14,2, 365–377, 1984.

apy. These four types are diagramed in Figure 9-1. These ethnic family maps are obviously stereotyped but they include common patterns which are typically seen in these families. They include (1) The matriarchal Irish family where mother is central and in control and father distant and infantilized; (2) the enmeshed consensual-democratic Jewish family, (3) the patriarchal, multigenerational enmeshed Italiam family with the mother as the heart of the family; and (4) the disengaged, independent WASP family.

Irish Families

The Irish American family with an alcoholic member and its specific therapy needs have been described in greater detail than other ethnic groups. Irish American families tend to view therapy in the same way they view confession: relating sins and gaining forgiveness (McGoldrick 1982b). Yet if the therapist uncovers their sins, they will feel embarassed. They are not assertive and do not let the therapist know if they are inconvenienced or uncomfortable. Because of their politeness and loyalty they may comply with the therapist without really changing. They view the therapist like a priest/authority and thus will respond best to a structured, problem-oriented approach or to a specific, clearly spelled out plan such as behavioral therapy (McGoldrick 1982b). Bowen's systems therapy (Bowen, 1974) may work well because of its respect for individual and subsystem boundaries. Irish families may also respond well to paradoxical techniques which encourage change without exposing inner feelings.

Irish families rarely seek therapy on their own, so court-mandated therapy for a substance abusing adolescent or an alcoholic father is a very common reason for referral. This is an embarassing situation for the family. Involving a distant father is often essential to correcting a maternally dominated imbalance. Some Irish fathers have become so totally removed from the family that it has been impossible to get them to come into therapy. Adolescent males identify strongly with their fathers although this concept is very alien to the teenager and difficult to accept. With the help of other family members, this identification with the father can be pointed out and the teenager helped to discard his extreme emotional distancing. Though the actual therapy may be very uncomfortable for these families, a deep sense of personal responsibility leads them to continue therapeutic work on their own after termination of formal therapy.

Jewish American Family

There is a very strong family orientation in these families, with marriage and children central (Herz & Rosen, 1982). There is also a strong sense of family democracy, with consensual decision making and diffuse generational boundaries (McGoldrick, 1982a). They place a high value on verbal explanation and reassurance in child rearing and don't use strong authoritarian directives or threats (McGoldrick, 1982a).

Jewish American families value credentials and education, and the therapist should not feel threatened by questions about these issues. When credentials are established, they readily consult with the therapist as a wise person, but still retain the right to make the final judgment about which interventions they will or will not use. They prefer complex, sophisticated interventions and consider behavioral types of techniques to be superficial (McGoldrick, 1982a). Talking and expressing their feelings is more important to Jewish American families than actively changing, and thus they prefer analytic techniques to strategic ones (Herz & Rosen, 1982). However, tasks are essential to shift from intellect to action, and they can be given in the families own complex terms, utilizing their language and rituals.

The therapist must respect the rules that support enmeshed togetherness at the same time as he or she facilitates some essential boundary making. This can be done by working with the more flexible parts of the system, such as the adolescent subsystem. They can be encouraged to accept less threatening parental gifts while they reject those which are infantilizing (Herz & Rosen, 1952). The therapist can readily join with the children in these families, without threatening the parents, because of their basic sense of democracy and egalitarianism (Herz & Rosen, 1982).

The Italian American Family

In Italian American families the family of origin has the highest priority, often creating difficulties for the spouse, who must cope with a mate's intense and exclusive ties to the family of origin.

Therapy with Italian-American families must focus on the renegotiation of their rigid system boundaries, which keep the extended family out of contact with the outside world (Rotunno & McGoldrick, 1982). They talk openly and with exaggerated feeling, yet hide their family secrets, which are plentiful. Secrets must be dealt with delicately, as their being make known to the therapist may constitute family betrayal (McGoldrick, 1982b).

The therapist must overcome being distrusted as an outsider, so that the authority necessary to change the family can be established. This may involve patiently surviving the family's many tests of the therapist's loyalty and skills (Rotunno & McGoldrick, 1982). Then the therapy can focus on helping the adolescent differentiate from the family in more adaptive ways than through substance abuse, yet permit them a face-saving way to remain within the family (Rotunno & McGoldrick, 1982).

Multiple family groups (Kaufman and Kaufman, 1979) can be very helpful in providing Italian families the support that they need to let their children individuate. Given the insularity of the Italian extended family, their willingness to open up and change in a group of other families is surprising. The use of an Italian co-therapist, their view of the doctor as respected expert, and other Italian families in the group who supported the letting go process were also helpful.

White Anglo-Saxon Families

White Anglo-Saxon families place a strong emphasis on independence, which extrudes children from the family early and neglects the extended family. They have difficulties in communication, are emotionally bland, and have an inadequate sense of self-worth, particularly when they do not meet the expectations of the Calvinistic work ethnic (McGill & Pearce, 1982).

In WASP families, the IP's difficulties are perceived as the patient's problem not the family (McGill & Pearce, 1982). Thus WASP families should be encouraged to stay involved, to provide support and to assume control of the problem. The substance abuser is encouraged to share his or her pain with the family so they are able to share the responsibility (McGill & Pearce, 1982). Since asking for help is so difficult for WASP families the therapist should support, rather than confront, these families in the early stage of therapy, and should build trust in order that their feelings of vulnerability will not be intensified (McGill & Pearce, 1982). Once the problem is clearly defined and a treatment contract is made, they will proceed with hard work in therapy, with the belief that this will be sufficient for success in therapy as it is in life. Thus they respond well to taking didactic courses. They are so understated that they may make significant progress in therapy or be deeply affected without telling the therapist. However, their lack of attachment makes termination of therapy an easy process (McGill & Pearce, 1982).

Black American Families

Although not included in Figure 9-1, this important minority's needs for family therapy are briefly discussed.

The constant impact of racism and discrimination is a continuing and pervasive aspect of black family systems and is a crucial factor in their family therapy. While females head more black families than white families, the two-parent family is still the norm among blacks. However, there is more role flexibility among blacks, with black fathers playing a bigger role in child rearing and nurturing than white fathers (McGoldrick, 1982a). Disciplining of children is strict and direct, but the lack of positive support by social structures leads to a high incidence of substance abuse in youth. Talking-oriented therapy is not effective or acceptable in black families, particularly those that have become underorganized as a result of social pressures (McGoldrick, 1982a). In black families, structural therapy, which strengthens family organization while adding to its flexibility, is the most effective model.

Gender Variations

In view of the differences in the families of female substance abusers, family intervention strategies with women must differ from those for males. Unfortunately, relatively little research attention has been focused on the best patient–treatment match for either sex. Family therapy may be more essential for female alcoholics because of their reactivity to symbolic or actual losses of spouse and children. The therapist should not impose a stereotyped view of femininity on female patients, as this could intensify the conflicts that may have precipitated their drinking (Sandmaier, 1980). The therapist should be sensitive to the specific problems of women and women substance abusers in our society and address these issues in treatment.

Person (1983) summarized four reasons why women prefer a female therapist: the fear that men have sexist values, a belief that it is too easy and tempting to fool a male therapist and avoid problem areas, the wish to avoid erotic transference and/or countertransference and a strong desire to have a competent woman with whom to identify. Although these reasons appear to constitute a rational basis for having female therapists treat female substance abusers, there is no evidence at this time that female therapists are more effective with female alcoholic patients than are their male counterparts (Annis & Liban, 1980) nor that women fare any worse or better in treatment than men despite the lack of specific techniques to meet their individual needs.

Women substance abusers have special concerns about their children and child care. They question how the parenting role fits into their life and establish and confirm parenting skills. Many women have been victimized in a number of ways in the past, including incest, battering, and rape. Catharsis and understanding of these feelings may be essential before a woman can build new relationships or improve her present ties. We do know that female substance abusers have more affective disorders than males and that these must be dealt with. Antidepressant medication may be appropriate; however, antidepressants, particularly those with sedating effects, can be and often are abused (by members of both sexes) and must be prescribed judiciously. Interestingly, the presence of an underlying neurosis relates positively to prognosis in female alcoholics. Female alcoholics who complete treatment are more likely than males to have a good prognosis (Annis & Liban, 1980).

Stage of Substance Abuse and the Family

With the exceptions of Steinglass (1980), Jackson and Kogan (1963), and Kaufman and Pattison (1981), most studies of the families of substance abusers have not addressed the differential effects of various phases of substance use on the family system. After an initial phase of denial, but still early in a substance using career, families tend to overreact in an enmeshed and chaotic way to drug-related behavior, particularly during periods of intoxication and heavy use. Later on, there is usually more of a tendency to form a new family homeostasis (that excludes the I.P.). Unfortunately, some families may stay enmeshed with the IP and family members may be dragged down to severe depression and substance abuse themselves. Families may also cycle between disengagement and enmeshed reactivity. During reactive stages, boundaries must be marked to calm down the system. In disengaged families, trust and closeness need to be gradually rebuilt. However, the therapist must realize that repetitive cycles may continue whether the family is in therapy or not and that these cycles must be expected. This is a strong argument for longterm therapy as well as for maintaining a positive alliance after treatment so that the family can return as needed.

Life Cycle Stage and Family Therapy

The family therapy of an adolescent IP obviously will have a different focus from the therapy of a grandparent IP. The family therapy of a 15-year-old will be quite similar regardless of the substance being abused, whereas the treatment of a 45-year-old corporate executive alcoholic may be quite different from that of a 45-year-old heroin addict of similar age, because their individual styles and family systems have evolved so differently over a long period of time.

Family Treatment of Adolescent Substance Abuse

Fishman, Stanton, and Rosman (1982) have noted that adolescent abusers differ from adults in the following ways: less chronicity and severity, peer group involvement that is susceptible to parental influence, less criminal activity, and fewer involvements in extrafamilial systems. Families with an adolescent IP invariably experience difficulties setting appropriate limits on adolescent individuation. The major therapeutic thrust in these families is to help the parents to set limits together while permitting flexibility in family interactions. Fishman et al. (1982) stated that the therapy of adolescents should be much more structural than strategic, since the goals are an intact family with a restructured parental heirarchy. Thus techniques used with adolescents include reframing their behavior as competent so they can be trusted, or as voluntary and delinquent so it can be controlled. It may also be necessary to diminish parental control in order to lessen the adolescent's need to rebel.

Marking boundaries is very important. After I have observed the adolescent's interfering role in parental decision making during an actualization, I work with the parents to restrict the adolescent from such interference while respecting the adolescent's right to his or her privacy. I will often ask the adolescent to leave the room while the parents are agreeing on limits, to underline the importance of making such decisions without the adolescent's presence or influence. Once a decision has been made, the adolescent can participate in negotiations as long as an intergenerational coalition or triangle can be avoided. After several decisions have been made in this way, we are better able to evaluate the extent to which the system can maintain its boundaries outside of therapy.

One frequently occuring situation in these families is parental substance abuse, which may be more extensive than that of the adolescent. However, if the adolescent is clearly labeled "the problem" by the family, then it is very important that the family be given some relief from the IP's stated problem before the parent's problem is addressed. On the other hand, if the adolescent's problems are only a means to get the more seriously disturbed parent into the session and the family clearly labels the parent's problems as major, then primary parental difficulties can be addressed or even made a part of the initial treatment contract. When parents are dependent on drugs or alcohol it is very difficult for them to acquire appropriate parenting skills, so finding a system for abstaining becomes a very high priority in the treatment.

For a drug-abusing young-adult offspring, separation from the family is often a more desirable goal. To achieve this, the therapist must create intensity, escalating stress and other strategic unbalancing techniques. In dealing with older adults, the structural-dynamic techniques which were described in the beginning of this chapter are indicated.

The family therapy of a grandparent substance abuser is just beginning to be addressed. Here it may be critical to involve their children and grandchildren to facilitate the IP's entry into treatment. Once a substance-free state is achieved then the IP grandparent can work towards achieving or re-establishing an executive or consultant position in the heirarchy.

MY PERSONAL APPROACH TO FAMILY THERAPY

My approach utilizes the multitude of techniques to which I have been exposed for 25 years. Some of these techniques will be familiar to any given group of therapists and some will be quite new. The most unique aspect of my approach is the synthesis of several different (even seemingly contradictory) treatment systems. The use of varying techniques depends on the unique needs of each family and stems from my longterm committment to individualized treatment plans. My approach to individual therapy, though still very psychodynamic, has been greatly influenced by family therapy, particularly family therapy with only one individual present. My family approach incorporates psychodynamic techniques as well as strategic, structural, communications, systems, and behavioral methods. An important influence on my approach has been the prolonged and deep exposure to the complicated and unique characteristics of substance abusers and their families and their needs for certain specific principles as well as a wide variability in change techniques.

Another critical aspect of my approach, which has evolved from years of contact with recovering addicts and alcoholics in AA, is requiring a committment to a system for achieving abstinence, which involves AA, NA, Antabuse, Al-Anon, etc. The emphasis on a system external to family therapy per se may seem unique to the family therapist, who is not ordinarily involved in the family's ecosystem. Although many aspects of the system used to stop substance abuse are frequently a part of family therapy, this emphasis on treatment outside the family helps to cool down the overreactive system.

Some therapists may find it difficult to integrate psychodynamic approaches with the more directive restructuring techniques. Liddle (1984) has noted that model integration is a complicated, sophisticated, and challenging task, and cautioned against a wholesale blending of models without adequate concern for clarity and consistency. In our drive towards eclecticism and flexibility we must not lose sight of the need for an integrated theoretical system. Liddle warned against the therapist becoming a "technique junkie" who approaches the family with preconceived techniques and molds the family to those techniques. He suggests that specific therapeutic maneuvers will flow readily from the therapist's role, basic ideas about change, and concept of therapy. When the therapist is able to work in an integrated way, he or she is able to interact spontaneously and creatively with each family (Liddle, 1984).

I realize that many readers would prefer a "cookbook" presentation that provides a clear, fixed system of how and when to use the various therapeutic modalities. Unfortunately, this is not possible because of the enormous number of factors influencing the therapist's choice of techniques. I agree with Liddle that the most effective form of family therapy is PEMT—one's personal *evolving* method of therapy. Hopefully this book will provide help to modify substantially our PEMT with substance abusers and their families.

Psychodynamic family therapists like Skynner and Framo easily integrate structural techniques into their therapies. Structural, and more particularly strategic, therapists reject psychodynamic approaches because they interfere with spontaneity and their emphasis on the here-and-now. At times this synthesis of the two approaches has been difficult for me. Generally I prefer to change behavior with a task rather than an interpretation. However, when tasks and other directives are resisted, interpretations can help prepare a family to accept the former, particularly when each family member's role in the dysfunctional behavior is complimentarily pointed out. On the other hand, when interpretations are resisted, framing them in a paradoxical way may facilitate their acceptance as well as change behavior. Some families may readily accept psychodynamic interventions, while others respond best to structural or strategic techniques. Thus the therapist moves back and forth between various kinds of techniques depending on his/her own personality and style as well as the family's needs and responsiveness.

I term my system of family therapy structural–dynamic because it is a fusion of structural–strategic techniques with *psychodynamic* methods and emphasizes the therapist as an active, *dynamic* participant rather than a passive, neutral screen. Despite a substantial amount of success with this integrated approach, many families, particularly those with a single parent, will not improve in individual family therapy sessions. Some of these families do quite well with a multifamily approach (chapter 10).

—————————————————————————— REFERENCES

Anderson, C.M., & Stewart, S. *Mastering resistance: A practical guide to family therapy.* New York: Guilford Press, 1983.

Annis, H.M., & Liban, B. Alcoholism in women: Treatment modalities and outcomes. In O.J. Kalant (Ed.), *Alcohol and drug problems in women.* New York: Plenum Press, 1980.

Bowen, M. Alcoholism as viewed through family systems and family psychotherapy. *Annals of the New York Academy of Science,* 1974, *233,* 115–122.

Fishman, H.C., Stanton, M.D., & Rosman, B. Treating families of adolescent drug abusers. In M.D. Stanton & T.C. Todd (Eds.), *The family therapy of drug abuse and addiction,* New York: Guilford Press, 1982, 335–358.

Haley, J. *Problem solving therapy.* San Francisco: Josey Bass, 1977.

Herz, FM & Rosen, E.J., *Jewish families.* In M. McGoldrick, J.K. Pearce, and J. Giordono (Eds), Ethnicity and Family Therapy. New York: Guilford Press, 1982.

Jackson, J.K., & Kogan, K.L. The search for solutions: Help-seeking patterns of alcoholic families. *Quarterly Journal of Studies on Alcohol,;* 1963, *243,* 449.

Kaufman, E. The Application of the basic principles of family therapy to the treatment of drug and alcohol abusers. In E. Kaufman & P. Kaufman (Eds), *Family therapy of drug and alcohol abuse.* New York: Gardner Press, 1979.

Kaufman, E., & Pattison, E.M. Differential methods of family therapy in the treatment of alcoholism. *Journal of Studies on Alcohol,* 1981, *42,* 951–971.

Liddle, H. Five Factors of failure in structural-strategic family therapy: A contextual construction in S. Coleman (Ed.), *Failures in family therapy.* New York: Guildford Press, 1984.

McGoldrick, M., Normal families: An ethnic perspective. In F. Walsh (Ed). *Normal Family Processes.* New York: Guilford Press. 1982a.

McGoldrick, M., Irish families. In M. McGoldrick, J.K. Pearce, and J. Giordano (Eds), *Ethnicity and Family Therapy*. New York: Guilford Press, 1982b.

Minuchin, S. *Families and family therapy*. Cambridge, Mass.: Harvard University Press, 1974.

Minuchin, S., Fishman, H.C. *Family therapy techniques*. Cambridge, Mass.: Harvard University Press, 1981.

McGill, D., & Pearce, J.K. British families. In M. McGoldrick, J. Giordano, & J.K. Pearce (Eds), *Ethnicity and family therapy*. New York: Guilford Press, 1982.

McGoldrick, M., Giordano, J. & Pearce, J.K. *Ethnicity and family therapy*. New York: Guilford Press, 1982.

Papp, P. Paradoxical strategies and countertransference. In A.S. Gurman (Ed.), *Questions and answers in the practice of family therapy*. New York: Brunner/Mazel, 1981.

Rotunno, M and McGoldrick, M., Italian families. In M. McGoldrick, J.K. Pearce, and J. Giordano (Eds), Ethnicity and Family Therapy. New York: Guilford Press, 1982.

Sandmaier, M. *The invisible alcoholics: Women and alcohol abuse in America*. New York: McGraw-Hill, 1980.

Steinglass, P. A life history model of the alcoholic family. *Family Process*, 1980, *19*, 211–226.

Whitaker, C. Process techniques of family therapy. *Interaction*, 1977, *1*, 4–19.

Chapter 10

Multiple Family Therapy and Couples Groups

An interlocking system of groups provides an ideal setting for the family treatment of substance abusers. These groups may include families of origin, nuclear families, and couples. In addition, I have found it quite helpful to have separate spouse, significant other, adolescent, and children's groups. The therapist can decide which combination of groups will best meet the needs of each individual and the family as a unit. These groups may be used along with individual family therapy or may be sufficient themselves to facilitate a family's shift to a non-substance abusing homeostatic pattern.

One advantage of an interwoven system of family-oriented groups and other treatment approaches is that this system impacts the identified patient and his or her family in a multitude of ways on a daily basis. In addition to up to several hours of family groups twice a week, the alcoholic attends AA two to seven times weekly. Also family members regularly attend AlAnon and AlAteen groups in addition to family therapy. Thus, we achieve a multiple-impact approach to therapy which is usually sufficiently comprehensive to shift difficult families to a healthy substance-free condition.

MULTIPLE FAMILY THERAPY

Couples groups are a widely used modality (Kaufman & Kaufmann, 1977) in the treatment of substance abuse. Unfortunately, too many programs rely on this treatment method and overlook the importance of children and other significant relatives of the indentified patient. Multifamily therapy (MFT), on the other hand, permits the integration of other family members who have a role in perpetuating the substance-abusing system as well as the power to change that system. MFT is particularly helpful in single-parent families, as group support and surrogate families provide leverage for change that would be otherwise difficult to achieve. MFT forms a new supportive network, a family of families which offers an alternative to a network of substance abuse facilitators and substance abusers.

The therapeutic team must include a primary therapist who is experienced in group and family therapy and comfortable in large groups. There should also be at least one cotherapist, preferably a recovering or recovered substance abuser; male–female balance in the therapy team is also preferred. The multifamily group is an excellent modality for training therapists in the dynamics of families and the techniques of group and family therapy.

The multifamily group is a stimulating and rejuvenating experience for therapist, treatment program, and family. The therapists become parental figures for a host of families who become a single family network and, in ways, a single family. At the same time the therapists have a "child's" role in each family. However, the therapists must step away from emotional entanglement and be objective, always keeping in mind that a critical function is to be a supportive ally to every member of the group. Cotherapists permit a division of joining functions when it is impossible for the primary therapist to ally with everyone in the group. The therapists must be in control of the group and feel the right to interrupt any communication that is destructive or disruptive (Kaufman & Kaufmann, 1977).

The group is seated in a large circle with cotherapists distributed at equal distances to provide observation of the total group. Families sit together, and their seating arrangements are carefully observed as they usually follow patterns of family interaction. Family members may be asked to separate if there is a great deal of whispering or disruption. The group begins with everyone introducing him- or herself by name and role in the family. A group member will describe the purpose of the group, generally stressing the need for families to communicate honestly and openly. This description may emphasize the importance of understanding and changing the familial forces that have led to substance abuse, without placing blame.

Usually one family at a time is worked with intensively. The first family frequently is worked with for about an hour. The conflicts they focus on set the emotional tone and influence the topics discussed in the entire group. Many other families will identify with these conflicts, express feelings, offer support, and work on similar conflicts (Kaufman & Kaufmann, 1977).

The total group frequently functions as adjunctive family therapists. Usually family members take their cues from the primary therapists and will be appropriately confronting, reassuring, and supportive. At times a family's own needs prevent this and their anger at their substance abuser spills over onto other identified patients in the group. At other times a family's protective and possessive qualities may be inappropriately directed toward group members. Families also often share experiences and offer help by acting as substitute extended families to each other outside of the actual therapy hours. Many family members recognize problems in other families that they can readily apply to themselves.

The informal contacts that take place before and after MFT sessions are crucial. Therapists should mingle and interact during these times. Many pre-session contacts are excellent grist for the therapeutic mill. Post-group interaction may confirm insights and validate feelings or, on the other hand, may undermine therapeutic work if not monitored. The family of a substance abuser who leaves treatment should continue to attend group therapy to maintain their own personal growth and new roles and to encourage the IP to return to treatment. (They may also return at crisis points even when treatment has been considered a success.)

In the early phases of treatment, the families support each other by expressing the pain they have experienced through having a substance abuser in the family. The family's sense of loneliness and isolation in dealing with this major crisis is greatly attenuated by sharing the burden with other families. The means by which they have been manipulated are quite similar and are the beginning of a common bond. The family learns to see the reciprocal destructive aspects of interaction with the IP. Patterns of mutual manipulation, extraction, and coersion are identified and negated. Perpetuation of the IP's substance abuse and dependent behavior through scapegoating, distancing, protection, or infantilization is identified, and new methods of relating are tried and encouraged. Family members tend to feel guilty when the IP confronts them with their roles in the addiction cycle. If the therapist does not intervene, they will retaliate by inducing guilt or undermining growth and may ultimately pull the addict out of treatment. Many IPs who have difficulty with the demands of treatment will try to convince their families to protect them from the "evils" of therapy. Intervening in this system helps prevent many early "splitees." Many families are able to do this merely through group support. Others must learn to recognize and reduce patterns of guilt, provocation, and enmeshment before they can close the door to the cycle of symbiotic reinvolvement. Thus the mother of a young addict was able to state in MFT, "Yes, I thought I was protecting my child from jail and suicide by giving him money for drugs. Now I know that was what was killing him. To take him back before he has graduated would also be killing him, and I must not kill my child by taking him back now."

Many families learn to express love and anger directly for the first time in MFT groups. Deep emotional pain is expressed when appropriate, and other family members are encouraged to give support to such expressions rather than nullify or deny them. When families are emotionally isolated, encouraging the mutual exchange of physical affection is helpful. MFT is particularly helpful in providing the emotional support necessary for enmeshed parents to separate themselves from the IP. An example follows:

One mother who had several brief psychotic episodes, many of which were triggered by her addict son, experienced such an episode when her son left residential treatment. Nevertheless she was instrumental in his return. After she recovered, she returned to MFT and told her son in group, "I will not hold you to me anymore."

Actualizations are used to achieve structural change in MFT. In one group of alcoholic families, whenever his mother and father achieved unity in setting limits, their 14-year-old son split them apart by bringing up how much his dad's previous alcoholic behavior was like the kids' acting out. This would provoke an escalating argument between them about "old tapes," and the children would go without needed limits. When this pattern was pointed out, the parents were able to resume appropriate limit setting for their son.

In later phases of MFT, families may express intense repressed mourning responses, over the loss of a substance-abusing member which are essential to a healthy adaptation. Family secrets and myths are also revealed in the later phases of MFT. When the anxiety stirred up by early shifts has been resolved, more advanced tasks can be assigned. In the final phases, the family and the IP deal with their separation from the group. Some families may continue contact with one another after leaving the group and may replace the entire network of the substance abuser with a new therapeutic network.

COUPLES GROUPS

Many of the basic principles of multifamily groups apply to couples groups. Couples groups solidify the boundary around the marital dyad and permit couples to work on their problems without interference from other members of their family and network. Frequently, issues worked on in the couples group can be subsequently tested in the multifamily group. The support of other couples who attend both couples and MFT groups helps the spousal pair follow through with their contracts and alliances and better deal with other family members. Couples groups should never be the only family treatment modality offered, because they neglect the essential three-generational model.

Couples groups are generally smaller than multifamily groups, consisting of three or four couples. Somewhat larger groups are often seen in inpatient settings. Couples groups are more common in outpatient settings and private practice than is MFT, perhaps simply because they involve fewer people and require less space. Couples sessions are also shorter, conforming more to the traditional group therapy period of 90 minutes, but more longterm, about 6 months to 2 years. The techniques used and phases elaborated in couples groups are quite similar to those in MFT.

The discussion of alcohol or drug intake is minimized in couples groups, and the focus is on six major issues: control, money, sex, intimacy, communication, and children. Couples are taught how to fight creatively and how to resolve conflicts involving these key issues. The group helps the couple "exhume" tender feelings that previously existed but have been buried in the family strife.

Sex is much easier to deal with in a couples group than in multifamily groups. For many couples, sex has become a source of manipulation and pain rather than pleasure (Kaufmann & Kaufman, 1979) because substance abuse and dependence diminish sexual drive. Sexual communication must be developed slowly.

Difficulties often arise in couples groups because the recovering abuser has given up the most precious thing in his or her life (alcohol) and expects immediate awards. The spouse, on the other hand, has been "burned" too many times and is unwilling to continue to provide awards. We encourage spouses to begin to trust and reward each other at the same time as we ask dry alcoholics and drug abusers to reevaluate their expectations of their spouses.

As a couple learns to get pleasure from their own relationship, the use of children as a battlefield diminishes. The generational distance between them and their children becomes appropriate and realistic. They also begin to separate themselves from their own families of origin (Kaufmann & Kaufman, 1979). The pronoun "we" begins to be used more and more, especially when couples deal with problems with their children. They are often amazed at how easy it is to manage the children when they themselves are in agreement. From this they develop constructive ways to talk to each other about the children and, consequently, their general communication improves. Longterm members of couples groups are alert to covert alliances between parents and children and readily point these out to each other. New members become increasingly aware that, as a couple, they are the center around which the family revolves. As long as these two feel good about themselves and each other, problems with the children are usually minimal.

For further details on couples groups, the reader is advised to consult Framo (1976) and Cadogan (1979).

SPOUSAL AND SIGNIFICANT OTHERS GROUPS

Many family therapists who do not specifically work with substance abusers might question the need for separate groups for the IP and the significant others. It is our experience that such groups are quite important on their own in addition to being part of the multiple impact on the family. Long before the advent of family therapy, group therapy (in the form of Alcoholics Anonymous) had emerged as a highly successful modality for the treatment of alcoholics.

Co-alcoholic and significant others groups are necessary to deal with the special problems of living with a substance abuser as well as to facilitate personal growth in the individual for alcoholic families, AlAnon and Alateen also facilitate an attitude of loving, detached acceptance. Ablon (1974) stated that the chief dynamic of the group process of AlAnon "is a learning experience resulting from a candid exchange and sharing of reactions and strategies for behavior related to living in a household with a problem drinker." The experience of others provides a basis for comparison and a stimulation of self-examination leading to a new insight in all areas of life experiences. However, Alanon is frequently not enough for the spouse, perhaps because the approach is not sufficiently individualized to deal with all the unique needs of the spouses of alcoholics. A common problem is finding an appropriate AlAnon group for male spouses, many of whose problems are different from those of the wife of a male alcoholic or who evoke strong reactions to mates that are not generally dealt within the AlAnon groups. A person married to an alcoholic who continues to drink or who drops out of treatment is encouraged to continue in his or her own group. The alcoholic may then later gain enough personal strength to return to treatment with a full commitment (Kaufman, 1982).

GROUP THERAPY FOR THE SUBSTANCE ABUSER*

At times the principles of reconstructive group therapy may be antithetical with those of AA. The "high support, low conflict, inspirational style" (Brown & Yalom, 1977) of AA and similar groups may inhibit attempts to uncover underlying affects and conflicts, yet the support may be necessary to maintain abstinence. The beginning group therapy for substance abusers should be educational, directive, and supportive and should impart knowledge of alcohol and drugs as well as coping skills to deal with the anxiety and depression inherent in stopping use. In the middle phases of group therapy, substance abusers work through feelings, responsibility for behavior, understand interpersonal interactions, and recognize the functions and secondary gains of their behavior. They become able to analyze defenses, resistances, and transference (Fox, 1962). The success of this middle phase depends on the substance abuser developing the ability to relieve anxiety without alcohol and drugs. In this vein, it is important not to end a session with members in a state of unresolved conflict (Blume, 1978). This can be avoided by bringing closure when troubling issues are raised. Closure can be achieved by the group's concrete suggestions for problem resolution. When this is not possible, group support, including extragroup contact by members, can be offered. By the closing phase of group therapy the substance abuser has accepted sobriety without resentment and is continuing to free her- or himself from underlying neurotic and characterologic problems (Fox, 1962).

In free-standing group therapy, substance abusers tend to become quite dependent on the group despite apparent intrap-

---

*For a more detailed discussion of group therapy techniques—see also Chapter 6, pages 87–103.

sychic gains. When the therapy is integrated with family therapy, termination is much easier, as dependency needs are gratified by spouse and family and giving is mutual. When group therapy is performed in the context of individual family therapy and family groups, the therapist is always performing family therapy with each individual in the group at the same time as other group techniques are used (Kaufman, 1982).

A TYPICAL MFT SESSION

This session which took place at Su Casa, a residential therapeutic community (TC) which is located on New York City's lower eastside, demonstrates a fusion of TC techniques and structural dynamic family therapy (Kaufmann & Kaufmann, 1979).

The 10 families and 3 therapists (over 40 individuals altogether) were grouped in a circle. Each person introduced him- or herself, stating name and role in the family or the group. A group member described the purpose of the group, emphasizing communication and confrontation of feelings. In this group, four families were worked with intensively, but the remaining families identified strongly with them.

The first family worked with consisted of the IP, who was a 27-year-old Italian male, and his older brother, mother, father, and wife. The mother dominated the family and their communications. The father was crippled and unable to work, and the mother had assumed the financial support of the family. It emerged that the father did not take care of his physical health because of worry over his addict son. The group pressured the father to make a dental appointment, and when he was vague, they exerted pressure on him to make a firm commitment, which he did. The son experienced guilt and began to cry, stating that he still needed his father. His mother cried in response to her son's tears and the three of them embraced. We learned that the IP, his wife, and his son were used to eating most of their meals at the mother's house prior to treatment. The wife and child were still eating their meals there during the week, and all of three of them during weekend passes from the TC. The wife and child were given the task of eating most meals at their own home during the week and three out of four weekends.

The mother and father readily agreed to reinforce this individuation. The IP and his wife embraced, bringing tears to the eyes of most group members.

The next family on which we focused consisted of a 23-year-old resident and his mother, and father. This family was also Italian. We worked with them to consolidate an insight from a previous session. The parents had devastatingly insulted their son but denied doing so. We therefore showed the sequence on videotape to break through the denial. They then accepted that they had devastated him, and, in getting in touch with their anger at him, they were able to refrain from putting him down in this session. The group also pressured the family to involve their drug-abusing daughter in therapy.

A third family consisted of the identified patient, who was a 34-year-old Irish male, and a younger sister and brother. The mother had been quite active in MFT but did not attend this session because the family had moved further away. The father had never been present but was frequently discussed because of his pattern of severe withdrawal. The father had not left his bedroom in three years and never came out when his son visited. In this session the son realized how much he had identified with his father's emotional isolation, even to the point of duplicating his posture. He was helped to recognize and experience this rigid control system. His anger toward his father would be a subject for future group work. He also realized how he had attempted to be a "father" to his younger siblings to the point of neglecting his own needs. The sister reached out to him and partially broke through his isolation with her poignant plea for adult intimacy. At this point another resident began to sob about not being closer to his own sister. He was asked to talk to the first resident's sister as if she were his own. In doing so, he reached a deep level of yearning and anguish. His mother reached out to him and began to rock him. To diminish the infantilization, the therapist asked the mother to not rock him. Freed from his mother, he was able to sob heavily about missing his sister and his guilt in pushing her away. We then returned to the Irish family but were still unable to break through the IP's emotional isolation. It was pointed out that it was difficult for him to express feelings because of his identification with his father and his need to stay in the role of the big brother who had no weaknesses.

Unfortunately, this man repeated his family role in the TC and became a leader before he had worked through his own problems. Several months later he used drugs again and had to begin the program again from the beginning so he could recognize and meet his *own* needs rather than assuming a caretaking "parental sibling" role.

CASE DESCRIPTION OF INTERWOVEN FAMILY GROUP THERAPY

Interwoven family groups consist of a network of several groups including members of several families. These groups include individual family assessment, a weekly group of alcoholics, a similar weekly group for co-alcoholics (significant others), a bimonthly multifamily group, and a weekly couples group.

This program requires only 3 to 6 hours weekly yet is quite comprehensive. Interwoven family therapy will be described as it involved the Johnson family.*

Kate Trent Johnson called to make the appointment, stating she was in a masters program and had heard about me from a fellow student. She knew I worked with families of alcoholics and thought I could understand her family because her husband, Dave Johnson, was an alcoholic who had been sober for 3 years.

Kate had been born in a small midwestern town. She was the middle of three children. Kate's father was an accountant who owned his own business, and her mother helped run the busines. Kate saw herself as being the "responsible one" of the children. She recalls feeling that she never got enough recognition for being so responsible.

---

*Pseudonyms and slight alteration of identifying data are used to protect confidentiality. This case is described in detail in E. Kaufman (Ed.) *Power to change: Family case studies in the treatment of alcoholism.* New York: Gardner Press, 1984.

Neither of Kate's parents were alcoholic. She described her father as the affectionate one and her mother as dominating.

Kate was a good student but quit college in her second year because she became pregnant and married her boyfriend. This pregnancy produced twin girls. Kate's third daughter was born when the twins were 15 months old. Her fourth child, a boy, came 13 months later and the fifth child one year after that. Kate had her "hands full" but she loved living in the suburbs and felt content with her babies. Her husband traveled quite extensively, leaving her alone with the children.

After one such trip, Kate's husband unexpectedly became quite angry at Kate and their only son. Kate had to rescue the boy from his father, who had become physically abusive. Among other things, her husband did not like the fact that she was now enrolled in a college program with the intention of completing her degree.

A turning point came when Kate's father got sick and died suddenly. She went home for the funeral, and her husband got angry because she spent money for the plane ticket. When she returned from the funeral her husband began insulting her father's memory. This was the last straw, and Kate asked for a divorce. They separated on and off for 6 months. Her husband fought the divorce. Finally after 3 years the divorce became final. Kate suffered deep guilt over the divorce and began to use tranquilizers and alcohol regularly. She felt under great pressure, and finally consented to give her ex-husband custody of their 5 children, as he had remarried by this time. When Kate was about to graduate from college 2 years later, he husband asked her to take back the twins, now 14 years old, and Kate agreed.

Shortly after graduation Kate met Dave, when she went to work for the company he worked for. She was attracted to him from the start. Dave was drinking at this time, but it did not seem to affect their relationship. They dated for 8 months and got married. At the time of their marriage, Kate had custody of the twins and Dave had custody of two of his boys.

Dave was 48 years old when he entered treatment. He was born in Portland, Maine, and was the oldest of four children. His parents separated when he was 12, and Dave became the man of the house. He dropped out of school in the eighth grade and started to drink while supporting the family by playing pool.

Dave and his family moved to California in 1951. He was drafted into the Army in 1953 and did very well. Although still drinking heavily, he married, graduated college, and began to climb the corporate ladder. Dave and his wife had seven children in a marriage that lasted 17 years. He described his first wife as "lacking in capacity for intimacy and hard to talk to." Dave had many extramarital affairs and experienced a lot of guilt as a result. They finally divorced because of these problems.

Dave described his and Kate's early relationship as being based on their being good drinking partners. After two years, their drinking became a major problem. They were "screaming and fighting" and were both "emotional wrecks." Soon, Dave was drinking around the clock and Kate was fearfully hiding from him. Dave entered a hospital alcohol program for a four-week stay but left after one week. He entered AA and submerged himself in the program once a day for 60 days, and then at least four times a week for about a year. He had maintained once-weekly contact with AA for 3 years prior to entering treatment and was committed to sobriety.

At the time they entered treatment, Kate and Dave had been married for 6 years. Three children from each of their prior marriages were living in the household, and several of the children's "mates" were constantly in the house. Five of the six children were between ages 16 and 19, and the last child was 13.

Dave and Kate focused on two problems in therapy: their children, and Kate's drinking. They had attempted to establish a contract that all of the children belonged to both of them, which they were unable to enforce. Kate's children came to her for controversial requests, and she gave in, as did Dave with his children.

Kate admitted to drinking one to four glasses of wine at night, five nights a week, a pattern which she had resumed two years before entering treatment. Dave didn't quibble about the quantity of wine but focused on her behavior when she drank. He stated that her speech slurred and her personality changed after one drink and that she responded to his confronting her about her drinking by drinking more, which in turn led to an argument. He admitted that he had been driving her to the store to buy wine, but had stopped because her drinking was worsening. I ended the session by asking Kate to deal with her drinking problem by resuming attendance at AA meetings at least twice a week (because she was not ready to attend more frequently), and asked Dave to leave Kate's drinking to me. Kate was a bit shocked that I focused on her drinking rather than Dave's alcoholic history, and we joked about the switch as well as her own recognition of a drinking problem. Fortunately, I had joined with her sufficiently that she agreed to work on her drinking, and they both agreed to come back with all 6 children who were living with them in four days.

All the children were handsome, bright, athletic, and articulate. Each child supported the idea that there were too many arguments and that a clear problem was the "blood parent" taking sides against the spouse's children. They also all supported the idea that Kate's drinking was a problem and that arguments were much worse when she drank. I assigned Dave to spend 15 minutes three times a week with each of his two older sons, from whom he had become distanced. He agreed to this and to the idea that if Kate didn't drink, he'd feel more supported in the family and could control his excessive shouting. The family all agreed to participate in family group; and they began that program the following week.

The Early Phase of Family Group Treatment

Kate and Dave made a great first impression in the group with their intelligence, sophistication, and attractiveness. Dave immediately emerged as a powerful figure contrasted with Kate's passivity and pliability. They were both extremely well liked by the group from the first meeting, and this feeling continued throughout their treatment.

Dave was prone to lecturing, and when he lectured her, Kate would cry. We used a directive approach to deal with this problem. We made each of them aware of their behavior. We gave Dave the task of stopping his parental lecturing and asked Kate to hold back her tears and express her differences directly. In the first half of the evening the group was divided into two segments: the alcoholic and the co-alcoholic group. We placed Kate in the alcoholic section and Dave joined the co-alcoholics.

When separated from Dave, Kate's anger surfaced. She was also able to recognize and verbalize her fears. In the weeks that followed, Kate began to realize that she had been running away all her life. Kate's fear of rejection was rooted in her own sense of inadequacy and weakness. She feared that one day she would become too weak to function and Dave would leave her. She saw no way out of her passivity and fear except to drink or to take tranquilizers. A major treatment goal was to find alternative solutions to deal with this dilemma.

In his group Dave seemed comfortable being the only male. He was ill at ease discussing emotions in front of women. Dave felt that expressing feelings was weak. He attempted to stay on an intellectual level. He knew he both provoked and supported his wife's drinking, yet he had difficulty changing these behaviors.

The groundwork for their growth started in their separate groups. Kate discovered her fear of rejection, and Dave began to discover the power of his emotions. When they were together in the combined group, Kate began to take risks by confronting and challenging Dave's authority. On the surface, Dave seemed to be supportive of this more assertive Kate, and verbalized that assertion was one of his goals for her. As Kate approached this goal, however, Dave became confused and uncertain of his role. Kate's risk-taking was forcing the relationship off balance. Dave seemed to be scrambling to get it back on the track. At this point, Dave's conflict was that while he "loved" having his wife sober and strong, he didn't know how to handle the changes.

The multifamily sessions also emphasized the split between Kate and her children versus Dave and his. However, another important coalition appeared in this group: a coalition by gender. Thus, Kate and all the female children were on one side, and Dave and the male children were on the other side. This appeared to be generated by Kate, who subtly encouraged this rivalry as an acting out of her hostility towards men. The children from both sides of this family became closer in the group. They asked for and received support from each other and gave a lot of support to the children of other families.

We also worked on the general problem of chore allocation, which was a very prominent issue with every family with teenage children. The families chipped in to decide what level of chores was fair for each child in the Johnson family and then applied these principles to their own family. As a result, the Johnson family developed their own regular family meetings at home for problem resolution.

Middle Phase

Kate continued to act more assertively with Dave at home. However, she told the group of a dream that confirmed her struggle and her growth: "I'm being chased by a few people with pointed objects. I'm scared and I run and run until I come to a house. I run in and make sure all doors are tightly locked. The people poke the pointed objects through the door. I feel scared but somehow I get hold of a knife and begin fighting back. I still feel vulnerable but I feel I'm fighting back and that feels better." We see by the dream that self-assertion is difficult for Kate because it has extremely frightening, life-threatening unconscious connotations.

Kate was now able to let Dave lean on her and be supported by her. This gave her what appeared to be a new identity in relation to him. She utilized this role of the supporter quite well. This was the first time we became aware of an important pattern in their relationship. If Dave felt strong, Kate had to feel weak. If Dave felt weak, than Kate could begin to feel strong by caring for him. She was attending AA about once a week at this time. We had encouraged her to attend on a more regular and frequent basis, but she was still very resistant because going to AA meant giving in to what Dave wanted her to do, which in turn deprived her of a source of inner strength independent from Dave.

Dave's insecurity and sense of inadequacy surfaced one night when he cautiously began to discuss some employment problems. The group therapists applied heavy pressure on Dave to give exact details. It became apparent that he felt something awful had happened, but he did not want to risk the loss of his image by admitting what it was. Finally, close to tears (for the first time), he told the group he had made an error at work and was close to being fired. The admission made him less perfect and more human to the group. The group was instantly supportive and Dave received the emotional nurturance that he needed. Dave stated that this was the first time he ever trusted his emotions enough to share them with a group of people. The sudden knowledge that he could do this safely changed Dave's life. The job crisis gave Dave permission to show the group and Kate his vulnerability. The group was able to give Dave the message that he was okay and that to feel vulnerable is not to be weak.

Dave applied for other jobs and found that he was sought after. He began to believe that he really was good at his job. This knowledge, plus the group's unconditional acceptance and Kate's total support, gave birth to a congruent self-image. For the first time in his life, Dave was beginning to feel like a complete human being. He became less rigid and more relaxed, dressed more casually, and exhibited less need to dominate the group.

As Dave became more relaxed, Kate became able to discuss sensitive issues more easily, and finally began to enjoy the group. However, simultaneously as Dave became more confident with his new self, he again became too strong for Kate and she started to feel weak and helpless. She drank for the first time in three months and Dave became furious at her and exaggerated her hangover symptoms. Kate responded seriously with, "I guess I should just do as he says," but she continued to drink during the ensuing Christmas holidays, becoming intoxicated on two occasions. Dave worked on reacting with loving detachment, stating, "I'm not going to say she's an alcoholic. She will have to find out for herself. I love Kate sober. I don't like the person she becomes after a few drinks." It was quite clear by this time that when Dave was feeling strong, drinking was the only way Kate felt she could maintain any sense of her own autonomy. However, this backfired and made her feel more weak and dependent. When this was pointed out to Kate, she responded by drinking in a controlled manner for several months. Dave did not overreact to her continued drinking but communicated his firm disapproval.

Termination

Dave continued to be too strong for Kate, which she dealt with by manipulating him into agreeing to terminate treatment. This move surprised the group, who disagreed with their decision but the couple was adamant. Although they terminated from the group, the Johnsons continued in a combination of individual, group, and family therapy for two additional years. Kate met another man with whom she felt quite strong and for whom she wanted to leave Dave until her new strength balanced the relationship and she left her lover to return to Dave. Eventually this strength waned and she left Dave again. Once apart from each other, their needs drove them together once again and they renegotiated their relationship in a conjoint session. Dave had sufficient self-confidence that he no longer needed to control Kate. Kate by now had a Masters degree in psychology and both she and Dave were working as group therapists for alcoholics and their families. I expect that the seesaw pattern of their relationship will continue for years to come but that they will settle on a more mutually balanced position.

The Johnsons are an example of the complicated healing process that can take place in an interlocking system of family and individual groups. Although Kate's substance abuse problem was primarily alcohol, like many middle-class women she also abused tranquilizers simultaneously or interchangeably. This case history and treatment is fairly typical of prescription drug abusers as well as of alcoholics and alcohol abusers.

—————————————————————————— REFERENCES

Ablon, J. AlAnon family groups. *American Journal of Psychotherapy,* 1974, *28*(1), 30–45.

Blume, S.B. Group psychotherapy in the treatment of alcoholism. In. S. Zimberg, J. Wallace, & S.B. Blume (Eds.), *Practical approaches to alcoholism psychotherapy.* New York and London: Plenum, 1978.

Brown, S., & Yalom, I.D. Interactional group therapy with alcoholics. *Journal of Studies on Alcohol,* 1977, *38*(3), 426–456.

Cadogon, D. Marital group therapy in alcoholism treatment. In E. Kaufman & P. Kaufmann (Eds.), *Family therapy of drug and alcohol abuse.* New York: Gardner Press, 1979, 187–200.

Fox, R. Group psychotherapy with alcoholics. *International Journal of Group Psychotherapy,* 1962, *12,* 50–63.

Framo, J.L. Family of origin as a therapeutic resource for adults in marital family therapy: You can and should go home again. *Family Process*, 1976, *15*, 193–210.

Kaufman, E. Group therapy for substance abusers. In M. Grotjohn, C. Friedman, & F. Kline, (Eds.) *A handbook of group therapy*, New York, Van Nostrand, 1982, 163–191.

Kaufman, E., & Kaufmann, P. Multiple family therapy: A new direction in the treatment of drug abusers. *American Journal of Drug and Alcohol Abuse*, 1977, 4(4), 467–478.

Kaufmann, P., & Kaufman, E. From multiple family therapy to couples therapy. In E. Kaufman & P. Kaufmann (Eds.), *Family therapy of drug and alcohol abuse*. New York: Gardner Press, 1979.

Chapter 11

Case Histories

These family therapy case histories deal with progressively severe identified patients according to extent of substance abuse. The first case history will deal with a "dry drunk;" the second with sibling teenage marijuana abusers; and the third with a heroin addict.

A "DRY DRUNK" FAMILY*

A "dry drunk" is someone who stops drinking and/or using drugs but continues to act in the same immature manner and maintain the same immature role in the family as when abusing substances.

Paul and Sandy Martin* were referred to me by their former family therapist on the East Coast, whom they called for a referral after being out of treatment for about two years. Paul was drinking alcoholically at the time he entered treatment with that therapist, but he had been sober for the past 3 years as a result of both the prior therapy and an active commitment to Alcoholics Anonymous. Sandy had been in a women's group

---

*Pseudonyms are used and specific life situations altered slightly to preserve cofidentiality. This case history was described by the author in more detail in E. Kaufman (Ed.). *Power to change: Family case studies in the treatment of alcoholism.* New York: Gardner Press, 1984.

with that therapist in addition to couple's therapy, and had made many recent steps toward personal growth in business and academics.

Paul and Sandy had grown up in the same East Coast city where I had spent my first 24 years and I recognized their accent immediately. I shared this with them, as well as the fact that I had been a member of my high school debating team, which had successfully defeated Paul's school's team, although his school's team eventually won the city championship that year. Paul and I teased each other about this, and joining with him through teasing helped establish and maintain our relationship throughout the therapy. Sandy and I joined through discussing her former therapist, with whom we both felt close.

Paul's and Sandy's interests, politics, hobbies, and jobs were as different from one another as were their physical appearance with Paul overweight and Sandy trim.

I took a brief family history from them in the form of a genogram. Both Paul and Sandy had strong family histories of alcoholism. Sandy's father had died four months prior to their entering treatment with me, though his death was not directly attributable to his alcoholism. Sandy had been married to a heroin addict for 2 years, who died from an overdose three years after their separation. John, now 16, was the product of that marriage and he presently lived with Paul and Sandy. Carl, 10 years old, and Steve, 12, completed the home. None of the children had serious problems. The younger boys, however, were described as provocative and Paul as overreactive.

Each partner was given the opportunity to specify the problems in the marriage. Sandy began by stating, "We're at the end of our rope. There is no intimacy or sharing. I can't give to him. I can't make a move to leave." I asked Sandy if her agenda for the therapy was to be able to leave. She responded, "If I can salvage our marriage, I'd like to try one more time." Paul agreed about the problems, but felt the relationship had a good chance for survival. Sandy stated, "If I'm going to be happy, I better find out now. If we continue to make each other miserable, I will not stay out of duty and loyalty. Paul gets wrapped up in everything else but me, no matter how trivial, and is very insensitive to me."

In the first session, we dealt with the effects on their relationship of Paul's AA involvement and the move to California. He found AA very important, providing an inner sense of homeostasis that was otherwise lacking. Sandy said she had felt abandoned when Paul went to a lot of meetings, but lately she liked the space when he was away. Sandy had attended AlAnon for 2 years as a precondition of her psychotherapy in Pennsylvania, but had not connected with AlAnon in California. Sandy was angry that Paul had made the decision to move to California without adequately consulting her. She was also angry because she felt he had ordered her to get a job to make money for food. However she enjoyed working, and her work created problems for Paul because he felt she was not sufficiently available to him and the children.

The session closed with a verbal contract that included the duration and cost of therapy, length of sessions, behavioral tasks, and the need for involvement of all three children. I included three tasks in the contract: Paul was to resume his active involvement in AA, and two specific step-study meetings were chosen to facilitate that work. Sandy was asked to resume attendance to AlAnon. In order to probe their capacity to shift their disengaged stance, they were both asked to plan a pleasant surprise for each other and not to talk about it until the following session.

The following session they reported that Paul had resumed more active AA involvement but Sandy had not gone to AlAnon. Sandy had taken Paul out to dinner, and Paul had taken her to Laguna Beach for an afternoon. Both surprises had gone well. During the rest of the session, they focused on their lack of closeness, for which they both blamed each other.

The children appeared for the third session. All three were verbal, expressive, and well-behaved. Paul and Sandy agreed that they were not "together" when it came to dealing with the kids, as they undermined each other on limit-setting. Sandy's overinvolvement with John, sometimes to the exclusion of Paul, Carl, and Steve, became obvious in this session, as did Paul's anger toward Sandy and his undermining of John.

I asked John to take the younger boys out to eat, underlining his adult competence and providing the parents a separate space from the children during the session in which to discuss an important spousal issue. I then told Sandy that her closeness with John had undermined and exluded Paul. I then complementarily confronted Paul, stating that his mistreatment of John had deeply affected his relationship with Sandy and that it was time he at least considered insuring John on their family policy, particularly if John bought his own car as he was planning. Paul agreed to discuss the possibility with his insurance agent. However, he procrastinated about this for several weeks. Finally Paul not only arranged for John's insurance at a reduced family rate but also helped John buy his own car.

Sandy was quite happy over Paul's giving attitude to John, and their relationship rapidly improved. However, they had a long-established pattern that whenever closeness developed, they would both get threatened and push each other away. I used the metaphor of a brick wall to describe the phenomenon, stating that when they were close to each other, it was like they had each taken a few bricks out of their protective wall. They then both feared that if another brick was taken away, their entire wall would crumble. I paradoxically suggested that they build up their wall again before it fell apart totally and landed on both of them.

Paul and Sandy always paid for therapy with two separate but equal checks. In subsequent sessions we dealt with the triangulation of their conflicts with money. Sandy felt that Paul controlled not only his money but also hers. One measure of his overcontrol was that all the bills were sent to a post office box so that he paid them away from home. They constantly bickered over who was responsible for paying for minor items and over Sandy's exclusion from major financial decisions. Sandy suggested that they work together on the distribution of their total income. Paul said that wouldn't work because he couldn't trust her. I told Paul that he treated Sandy like a slave about money and that she, like a slave, was constantly rebelling and undermining him. We then talked for several months about mutual decision making in financial areas. Paul in his usual fashion, objected and refused to compromise but ultimately he came around, including Sandy in a major financial decision.

Four months into therapy, we focused on Paul's hostile teasing of the two younger boys. I shared with him that it made me sad that he loved them so much but kept pushing them away. I then gave Paul the most tasks, by far, that I have ever given anyone in a session. There were 12 tasks in all, and most of them were ways for him to change so that he could relate better to his younger sons. These were called "The Twelve Steps to Paul's Happiness." (Taken from AA's 12 steps). This quantity of tasks and their "as if" quality is reminiscent of Stuart's caring days technique, described in detail in Chapter 8. They include several "here and now" directives:

1. Check your teasing of your two younger sons.
2. Do not bully them.
3. Do not get down to their level unless it is fun for them.
4. Express your love in a more direct way so that they feel it.
5. Be tender with Steve at bedtime in the same way you have learned to be tender with Carl.
6. Remember that Steve is not you, even though he is as stubborn as you.
7. Put yourself in a position so that you can be affectionate with Steve.
8. Ask Sandy for help if you are on the verge of blowing up at the boys.
9. Both you and Sandy should discuss decisions about discipline or limits, both should present them to the children, and both should implement them.
10. Diminish teasing Sandy and work on communicating directly with her.
11. Help with the dishes when you do not have an AA meeting.
12. DO NOT suggest to Sandy that she quit her job in order to solve the problems of the kids.

[To underscore the importance of this task, as well as to interject the type of humor that Paul responded to so well, this was called "number three." This task was restated that Paul should never again even mention "number three."]

Sandy was given four tasks:

1. Talk to Steve's teacher about a program for his school difficulties.

2. Serve dinner by 6:15 P.M., but preferably by 5:45 P.M. [to prove that Sandy could take care of the house even while working].
3. Do not side with John in a way that alienates Paul.
4. If Paul does 6 of his 12 tasks, he is to get a sexual surprise. In addition, if you do all four of your tasks, Paul is to give you a sexual surprise.

At the next session, they reported that they had done many of the tasks and felt so close that they both feared their walls were crumbling. Sandy had given Paul a sexual surprise and they both grinned contentedly about it (but they did not share the content with me). However, their major problem was still the extent to which they permitted John to get between them. It appeared to me that John's relationship with Sandy would continue to keep her and Paul apart as long as he lived in the house. He was old enough to leave, and for a number of reasons wanted to leave. I stated that it would be best for John and for the other four family members if John went away to school for his senior year to a place where he could learn the auto repair trade, in which he was very interested. Sandy responded tearfully, "You mean get rid of the kid."

The next session was three weeks later and Sandy reported an important insight based on the above intervention. She stated, "I married Paul to have a father for John. I had Carl so that Paul could learn to be a father for John. I've hung on to the idea that I could make the relationship better between Paul and John. This was jerky because I can't control Paul's reactions. After the last session, I gave up on that." I confirmed how important her insight was, stating, "You can't make Paul be John's natural father. He may become a father, but not the one you want him to be."

Sandy had received a promotion at work, but her car had broken down, requiring a month to be repaired. This made her dependent on her friends and on Paul, and she was quite angry with him. She was unable to ask him for help because she felt too vulnerable. She also felt that in order to have time with Paul, she had to beg and plead and she no longer wanted to make the effort. They were feeling particularly distant, and I related this to the stress of Sandy's not having her car. I pointed out that at times of external stress, they attacked rather than supported each other. I stated that they could not expect to build closeness again until the car problem was solved, which relieved the pressure they were feeling. Indeed, they did begin to build closeness once Sandy got her car back in working condition.

Six months into therapy, they reported that John had moved out of the house and was living with the family of a friend. The immediate move did not help their relationship, but rather stressed it still further. I stated that this was a very stressful time, but John's moving out could be very helpful to them if they did not let his ghost get in their way. We jointly worked out the initial steps necessary to facilitate this process. These included specifying the extent of Sandy's time with John, as well as John's contact with the other boys, and how to deal with the contents of John's room.

The following session Sandy made her first verbal "slip" in the therapy, calling John an "exterminated minor." I don't frequently use slips in family therapy but this one was too powerful to avoid. I pointed out that not only was Sandy mourning John's loss, but she was guilty about her own role in the "extermination" and was projecting the blame to Paul and then attacking him for it. Paul was now chasing Sandy for closeness. He was given the task of not chasing her, and she the task to let him in from time to time.

John began to get into difficulties that were new to him. He received a traffic ticket, necessitating that Sandy come to court, and he also began cutting classes. Sandy felt he was asking her to become reinvolved with him by setting limits and she decided to do so.

Sandy and Paul continued their cycle of closeness and hostile separation for several months, until Paul made a major compromise concerning the purchase of a safe car that was large enough to accommodate the entire family on a trip. The car was something Sandy had wanted for a long time. Paul was pleased at how warm and uncritical Sandy had become but was concerned about her maintaining this attitude stating, "I can't buy that many new cars."

Sandy said that she worried about the change because she had not worked for it and that Paul had made it all happen. I asked Paul what gave him the strength to do it and he replied,

"I'm stubborn." Sandy didn't understand his answer until I reframed it: "He's so stubborn, he'll even prove he can be wonderful to you." I closed the session with a reminder that the bricks were falling down rapidly and they'd better be cautious.

Two rather good months followed this turning point, augmented by the boys being away for the summer. At the end of this 11-month course of therapy, Sandy stated, "I felt close to Paul and didn't have to demand that he come closer. In the past, I could feel independent until it was necessary that we both agree. Now I feel more like we're a couple and that I can agree and still feel independent."

Discussion

Therapy with a family in as much conflict and so close to dissolution as the Martins were is always very difficult and demanding on a family therapist. However, there is a sense of exhilaration when things go well because they and you have worked so hard. When I begin therapy with a family that is just about ready to give up but unwilling to separate, I am aware that I will have to commit a tremendous amount of energy and effort, regardless of whether they choose to remain together or to separate. My present use of a more strategic approach puts less pressure on me as a therapist with couples like this, because more indirect techniques help me to feel less responsible. That is, I go with the resistance rather than oppose it strongly and directively.

Paul's 3 years of sobriety were a necessary building block to a good relationship with Sandy. Yet when they entered therapy with me, there had been little change in their basic patterns of relating for those same 3 years. If anything, Sandy's independence had driven them apart and caused more conflict. Despite his sobriety, Paul, like many sober alcoholics, had not learned to overcome his fears of intimacy or to share his wife with his family and his family with others.

Perhaps the key technique in working with this family was that of demarcating boundaries. A most important boundary that was repeatedly developed and strengthened in this therapy was the one surrounding Sandy and Paul and separating them from John. Several restructuring maneuvers were used to accomplish this. Building Paul's positive relationship with John was helpful because it lessened Sandy's need to join with John to protect him from Paul. Solidifying Sandy's ties with Paul lessened her need to stay enmeshed with John. Breaking the cycle of distance from Paul equals closeness to John allowed Sandy increased closeness with Paul. Sandy was unwilling to give John the transitional space he needed to pass from adolescent to young adulthood. Permitting John to become an autonomous young adult provided him with the space he needed and provided Sandy and Paul with needed protection from his interference in their relationship.

Most of these boundaries were established by tasks within the sessions and as homework. Although I used directive tasks mainly, I was also paradoxical at times. The Martins responded to my directiveness as often as they resisted. Rather than utilize a paradox when they resisted, I generally chose to become more emphatic and intense in my directives, to which they ultimately responded, often after several weeks of inactivity or resistance. I was able to achieve this because we were joined so well, and we continued to trust each other. I felt that the use of too much paradox would have broken this trust. When I utilized that paradox, as in asking them not to get too close too quickly because they needed the distance, I prescribed the reason why each person should continue their behavior in the symptom-producing cycle.

MARIJUANA ABUSE*

A family entered treatment because Milt, age 16, and his brother Doug, age 17, were arrested together for smoking marijuana in a car, and treatment was a part of their probation. I invited their family of origin to the first session. Sylvia, the mother and Tony, the father, both 37, sister Carol, 18, and

---

*This case history material is based on material used in Kaufman, E. Adolescent substance abusers and family therapy. In M. Pravder & S. Koman (Eds.), *Adolescents and family therapy.* New York: Gardner Press, in press.

brother Jimmy, 5, also attended. The teenagers' pot smoking was symptomatic of overall family and individual dysfunction. Sylvia had been in pyschotherapy for a year for a weight problem and difficulties in relationships. She was taking amphetamines for weight reduction and had been on them for an extended period of time. Tony was a moderately successful small-business owner who had difficulty asking for money that was owed to him, leading to frequent family financial crises. Carol was employed as a clerk and was on the verge of moving out of the house. Doug was described as having a personality change related to marijuana. He admitted to smoking up to 12 joints a week including during school hours. He had become passive and irritable but generally responded well to structure. Milt was much more assertive and had a very lucrative weekend job. He would involve the family in endless debates whenever they attempted to set limits for him.

Doug and Milt had signed a probation contract in which they agreed to not be out after curfew and to abstain totally from alcohol and drugs. Tony generally let his wife take responsiblity for every aspect of household and parental decision making. When she failed, he expressed extreme rage and made rigid restrictions, which he later failed to enforce. One solution that he had tried in the past was to have the boys work in his business, but this generally failed because of their defiance and his inconsistency in setting limits. Although Sylvia had most of the power in the family, she felt controlled by her husband.

I asked the parents to agree in this first session to establish clear limits about marijuana smoking. They came up with the following limits on their own: If they determined that one of the boys was smoking pot (and that judgment was to be strictly up to them), then that boy would work five days without pay and be placed on restriction for one week. If he was caught a second time, the penalty would be doubled, and if a third offense occurred, he would be asked to move out. The family was also asked to plan one meal a week that they would all eat together.

The family arrived for their second session with a suitcase full of Jimmy's toys. This helped focus the session on how the family interacted around the youngest child. Because of asthma, Jimmy slept in his parents' bedroom. This was focused on as a way of keeping the parents apart, and the first in a series of tasks to move him into Carol's soon-to-be-vacated room was assigned. When the family were asked to deal with getting Jimmy's toys packed when 15 minutes were left in the session, a typical family interaction was seen: The older sibs all put him down, saying he could never do it himself. Sylvia defended him while Tony began to put the toys back himself. Tony was asked to support his wife in requiring that Jimmy do it himself; neither parent was to do the job for him. Jimmy's interfering with his parents' closeness had to be dealt with, as well as the ways in which they undermined each other. If they could learn to deal together with Jimmy and reestablish their own intimacy, then they could better handle their teenagers. The teenagers were also asked to limit their parenting of Jimmy and leave these functions to his natural parents.

It required two months of gradual practical steps, such as choosing and hanging wallpaper, to move Jimmy into his own room. During this time, many emotional issues between the parents were also explored and they began to spend what they termed "quality time" together. Once they were able to function as a team sexually as well as in decision making, the teenagers' marijuana problems abated substantially.

The family functioned well for over a year after the termination of their initial course of therapy, but returned when they learned that Milt was again smoking marijuana and Carol was asking to come back home. At this point, their functioning was at a sufficiently high level for them to readily agree that Carol was not to come home because "she regresses and pulls the whole family back." They were also able to establish clear guidelines about their expectations for Milt, who was now 17½, and to state firmly that if he did not follow them, he would be requested to leave the house even if he was in college and functioning well. I supported their position, even though Milt's use of marijuana at this time was apparently not interfering with his functioning, because both parents were clearly together on this issue, and because parents have the right to place limits on the drug and alcohol use of children living in their own home, no matter what their age.

In this case example, substance abuse was relatively mild and the situation could be resolved by direct structural approaches including strengthening the spousal bond; removing the youngest child from interfering with his parents' relationship and from his overinvolvement with his mother; strengthening the husband's self-confidence; facilitating the daughter's moving out and staying out; and some normalizing of the older boys' behavior.

HEROIN DEPENDENCE IN A YOUNG
COUPLE*

This family consisted of Tom, age 19, his wife Cora, also 19, their 1-year-old son John, and Tom's family of origin: brother Mel, age 17, Tom's mother, June, a 54-year-old registered nurse, and his father, Jack, a 56-year-old engineer and rodeo afficionado. Julie, a 30-year-old sister who was living in the Midwest, joined us three weeks later for a pivotal session. Two older siblings were married and distanced from the family.

Tom and Cora had both used heroin since 14 and been addicted for over two years. They had both been on methadone maintenance since age 18. They had very lucrative jobs in which they were given a daily percentage of the money they raised for a charity. Tom had difficulty with the ready access of money. He fell behind in the amount he was to turn back to the company because he was spending huge sums of cash (over $200 daily) to inject sufficient heroin to overcome his methadone blockade. Cora would argue with him about his wasting the money. When he shared his heroin with her, however, she would stop protesting. Because of the money spent on heroin, Tom and Cora were unable to pay the fees of their private methadone program and were "borrowing" from Tom's mother to pay their weekly fees. June had been keeping Tom's money for him but he still managed to withold enough for heroin. He had also stolen goods from everyone in the family and pawned them. June would then pay off the pawnbroker and return the goods to the household. Her protectiveness of Tom caused constant conflict between her

---

*This case is based on material described in Kaufman, E. Addescent substance abusers and family therapy. In M. Pravder & S. Koman, *Adolescents and Family Therapy*. New York: Gardner Press, in press.

and her husband, Jack and reinforced their distance. Jack repeatedly threatened to kick Tom out but couldn't enforce it because of June's fears that Tom would die if he were outside of the family.

The therapist pointed out to June that her overprotectiveness kept Tom an infant while her constant concern with Tom kept her apart from her husband. She responded with, "I can't kick him out, what else can I do?" I suggested that a simple answer would be to ask her husband for help, but she was not ready to do this yet because they had become too used to being polarized. She suggested instead that she could send him to Phoenix House (a residential therapeutic community for drug abusors). I suggested that we evaluate the situation further. To do that, I would have a session with Tom, Cora, and John; an individual session with Tom (to join with him and work towards his being an ally in his own individuation): and a family session with Julie when she returned home for Christmas. (Christmas week is often a good time to hold a family session, as family members who have left the household are often around at this time.) I also assigned the parents the task of going out on a date the next time Tom got high on heroin.

In the session with Tom, Cora, and John, Cora tended to deal primarily with John, keeping Tom on the periphery. They revealed one of the typical patterns in co-addicted pairs: Cora would never initiate using heroin on her own but would only use it when Tom provided it. Tom was able to state that he knew his mother would always bail him out if he got into trouble and this was one reason he felt he could use heroin in safety. They also stated that all of their peer relationships were with fellow heroin addicts and felt this contributed to their problems. They were given a task to spend one evening with a drug-free couple and to keep in mind that this would be very frightening to them.

In the individual session with Tom, we explored his fears of success and independence as well as his guilt about manipulating his mother. We also discussed Julie, who had been seriously disfigured facially by a gunshot wound when she was 9. She received a great deal of attention around the wound and ten years of surgery to correct it. June felt guilty about the attention she gave Julie and tried to make it up to Tom. Tom denied that he was directly upset about Julie, stating that he did not use drugs until three years after her accident.

The session that Julie attended was very poignant because of her facial disfigurement and her inability to speak, yet she had a powerful presence. She communicated in writing. Her notes began with "I know what you're going through" and "I don't have anyone who can help me by saying I've been there." She wrote to her mother, "You're killing Tom and keeping me alive." She suggested that the family establish a written agreement of ground rules, which would permit them all to live together without conflict. When attempts at this faileld, she wrote her last note: "I don't think Tom can get out of his habit alone. I think he needs a residential program." The family readily agreed that Tom would enter Phoenix House and Tom agreed to go. I reinforced this by stating that I was pleased they had all agreed to this and that no further therapy was necessary at this time, but that I would apreciate a call about how Tom was doing at Phoenix House and how the family was doing in general.

Four months later, Tom called, requesting an individual session. He informed me that he had not gone to Phoenix House because it was "too much like jail." He had quit his job, which had solved the problem of having money available for heroin. His mother was now paying for his and Cora's new methadone program. However, he was now devoting himself to golf, which was a great pasttime of his father. Jack and Tom were playing golf together at least three times weekly, which was bringing them closer than they'd ever been. Unfortunately, Tom had pawned his golf clubs a few days before to obtain the money to buy heroin. This permitted us to focus on his self-destructiveness, as well as his fears of closeness and success. Since Tom had a "system" for staying off heroin, (methadone maintenance) and since he and his family expressed motivation for change, I agreed to resume outpatient treatment even though he had recently used heroin and they had reneged on their agreement to put him in Phoenix House.

I stated to the family that I had gone too fast the last time and that Tom's parents were not ready to part with him because they needed him around to occupy their relationship and keep them apart. They readily agreed with the first part of the paradox, seemingly not hearing that they needed Tom to continue his symptomatic behavior. I also suggested that both parents join AlAnon to help them learn to become less involveld with Tom as well as to have an activity which would unite them. Since re-entering therapy, Tom has remained free of heroin for 4 months and has registered for college. Cora has a job, but infuriated the family by stating that she wanted to buy an expensive ring before she paid off her debts to them. She is 5 months pregnant, and a new child will reinforce her and Tom's dependence on the family. Tom got his golf clubs out of hock with money earned from odd jobs. He has begun to explore his intense fear of his father and how the fear disappears when he and Jack play golf together.

Tom's stated goal, as well as that of every other family member, is for he, Cora, and John to leave the household and establish one of their own. In order to achieve this, the tie between Tom and his mother will have to be loosened further. Tom's new relationship with his father is an important step in that direction. However, his mutual ties with Cora will have to be strengthened, as will the ties between his mother and father. Tom and Cora's getting off of methadone is a longterm goal of this therapy, but neither expresses any motivation for detoxification at this point.

Discussion

Outpatient treatment was initially terminated to reinforce the family's decision for longterm residential treatment as the only apparent system that Tom could utilize to implement that decision. Four months after that termination, Tom and his family returned to treatment, this time at Tom's urging. With some realignment of the family, particularly Tom's alliance with his father, outpatient family, individual, and couple therapy had a better chance of being successful this time.

The initial intervention would have been more successful if I had available a multifamily group, which would support maternal letting go, or if the parents had attended AlAnon. However, unlike most of my work with the families of substance abusers, such a group was not available to me at the time this family participated in treatment. Without this type of support, I worked paradoxically with the family's need to hold on to Tom. Cora's pregnancy certainly reinforced Tom's need to stay at home for financial and reasons of convenience, offered their children more stable parenting through the grandparents. Although at this writing Tom remains free of heroin, he continues in a coalition with June, which prevents his growth. Julie will be moving nearby the family shortly and she may help provide needed leverage for the further restructuring necessary for Tom and Cora to set up their own household.

Chapter 12

The Future of Family Therapy of Substance Abusers

The future looks very bright for further developments in the family therapy of substance abuse, because of the many exciting recent developments in family therapy and the rapidity with which they are being applied to alcoholics and drug abusers. In addition, the study of family systems is becoming more accurate and valid, so we will shortly be seeing more reports of these families based on scientific study rather than anedoctal reporting or gross descriptions. To this end, the National Institute of Alcoholism and Alcohol Abuse (NIAAA) is funding several quantitative studies of family systems in alcoholics, the results of which will soon be available. Likewise, the National Institute of Drug Abuse (NIDA) has recently funded comparative studies of the efficacy of family therapy, the results of which should be made public in the late 1980s.

FAMILY SYSTEMS EVALUATION

Although there is a great deal of knowledge about family systems in substance abuse and there has been an appreciable degree of success with family treatment, there are still many unanswered questions.

There are two basic methods for evaluating family function: self-completed family questionnaires, known as the "insider's view," and an objective rating by a trained observer or "outsider's view" (Olson, 1977). The major types of self-report include Moos and colleagues' Bell & Portner (FES) Family Environment Scale (1974) and Olson's Family Adaptability and Cohesion Evaluation Scale, FACES I (1978) and II (1982). In addition, the brief family APGAR has been developed by Smilkstein (1978) and more recently, the Structural Family Interaction Scale by Perosa (1981). The FES and FACES have been most widely used. It is unfortunate that two such similar instruments are in such wide use, as a more unitary scale would give us a much broader range of families evaluated with the same instrument. As Moos (1982) has noted, these instruments can be used to predict useful treatment interventions as well as success. The family factors that predict better treatment response include greater cohesion and involvement in recreational pursuits, decreased conflict, control and disagreement, and more tasks performed jointly by both spouses.

Quantifiable evaluations by a trained objective observer are at an early stage of development. Olson (1982) has reported a great deal of difficulty in achieving significant inter-rater reliability in the Clinical Rating Scale (CRS) Olson (1980) and had to implement a retraining period in the use of this scale. Both Olson and I have noted that on the CRS the trained observer tends to evaluate the family as far more pathological than the family rates itself. O'Farrell and Cutter (in press) recorded videotapes of two 10-minute samples of couple interaction: first, a discussion of a current problem area in the marriage, and second, vignettes from the Inventory of Marital Conflicts. These interaction samples were coded by trained raters under Robert Weiss's direction at the University of Oregon Marital Studies Program using the Marital Interaction Coding System (MICS). This instrument evaluates couples' ability to reward rather than punish one another and the efficacy of problem solving. The use of videotapes saves time and effort in training raters and permits raters to score blindly in regard to treatment conditions and the hypotheses of the study.

A confirmation/disconfirmation scale developed by Sieburg (1969) can be scored by the families' self-reports, by an observer during the session, or by viewing a 10-minute videotape of couples' problem solving behavior.

Another neglected aspect of the evaluation of family systems and family treatment of substance abuse is the specification of the exact nature of the population in treatment so that studies can be compared.

When we are dealing with more than one individual, differences are mulitiplied exponentially. Thus we must consider social, psychological, and biological factors in every family member. For example, depression, bipolar disease, antisocial or borderline personality, or substance abuse in another family member (in addition to the IP) creates a much more complicated and difficult-to-treat family than one in which the only diagnosis that can be made is the alcoholism or drug abuse of the IP. Another critical issue is the contribution of ethnic and social mores of family dysfunction. In my own studies of the families of heroin addicts and alcoholics (see Chapters 2 and 3), the ethnicity of the family was shown to have an extremely powerful effect on family function and roles.

Still another factor is the psychopathology of other family members, particularly spouses. We are still not certain if spousal pathology precedes the alcoholic and drug abusing behavior or is a consequence of it, although the latter is the current favorite. We will not have a definitive answer to this question until we do prospective studies of psychopathology of all family members in high-risk and ordinary-risk families, using longterm follow-up. The roles of gender in substance-abusing families are just being explored (see Chapters 3 and 4).

DEMONSTRATION OF THE EFFICACY OF
FAMILY THERAPY WITH SUBSTANCE
ABUSE

Those of us who use family therapy know that it works. However, this knowledge is not sufficient proof of effectiveness. Most studies of the family therapy of substance abusers claim success, yet, to date, the methodology has been less than adequate. The entire field of family therapy is just entering a phase of scientific evaluation which, fortunately or unfortunately, will result in as rigorous an evaluation as individual therapy has had in its longer history. Certainly, similar questions can be raised about the efficacy of any system of psychotherapy presently in use.

Papers have been published on the success or failure of a single case in family therapy (Dinaburg, Glick, & Feigenbaum, 1975). These can be dismissed with the same ease as the clinician's own subjective perceptions. That single-case studies continue to be published emphasizes the relatively pristine state of family therapy evaluation. I will not attempt to thoroughly review the evaluation literature on family therapy of substance abusers. Stanton (1979) and Janzen (1977) have already provided excellent reviews of drug abuse and alcoholism, respectively. However, I will discuss several examples of family therapy evaluation in this field.

Silver, Panepinto, Arnon, and Swaine (1975) described a methadone program for pregnant addicts and their addicted spouses in which 40 percent of the women became drug-free in treatment and the male employment rate increased from 10 percent to 55 percent. Both rates are much higher than those achieved by traditional methadone programs without family treatment. The problem with this study, as with most evaluations of family approaches to drug abuse, is the lack of follow-up data or control groups. Ziegler-Driscoll (1977) reported a study conducted at Eagleville which found, on follow-up at 4 to 6 months, no difference between treatment groups that included family therapy and those that did not. However, the therapists were new to family therapy and the supervisors new to substance abuse. As the therapists became more experienced, their results improved. Stanton and Todd's (1982) project of family therapy with heroin addicts on methadone is perhaps the most outstanding family treatment and evaluation project to date with hare-core drug addicts. They compared paid family therapy, unpaid family therapy, paid family movie "treatment," and a control group with no family treatment. Follow-up 1 year after end of treatment showed that the two family therapy treatments produced much better outcomes than nonfamily treatments in abstinence from drugs. The nonfamily treatment and movie groups did not differ from each other. Hendricks (1971) found at 1-year follow-up that narcotic addicts who had received 5½ months of MFT were twice as likely to remain in continuous therapy than addicts who did not attend MFT. Kaufman & Kaufmann's (1977) work has shown that adolescent addicts treated with MFT have half the recidivism rate of clients without it. Stanton (1979) noted that of 68 studies of the efficacy of the family therapy of drug abuse, only 14 quantified their outcome, and only 6 of these provided comparative data with other forms of treatment or control groups. Four of these (Hendricks, 1971; Scopetta, King, Szapocznik, & Tillman, 1979; Stanton, 1978; Wunderlich, Lozes, & Lewis, 1974) showed family treatment to be superior to other modes. Winer, Lorio, & Scrofford (1974) and Ziegler-Driscoll (1977) found no superiority in family treatment. Stanton (1980), however, concluded that "family treatment shows considerable promise for effectively dealing with problems of drug abuse."

Although there has been more detailed evaluation of the family therapy of alcoholism than of drug abuse, Janzen (1977) stated, "It is not possible to show that family treatment is as good or better than other forms of treatment of alcoholism." However, he also stated that such treatment has advantages to the family and the alcoholic that other treatments do not offer. Despite their methodologic shortcomings, all the studies he cited reported positive results. Meeks and Kelly (1970) reported the success of family therapy with five couples, but no comparison group couples were included. They described abstinence in two alcoholics and "improved drinking patterns" in the other three, but no objective measures of family functioning. Cadogan (1973) compared 20 couples in marital group therapy with 20 other couples on a waiting list. After 6 months of therapy, nine couples in the treatment group, but only two couples in the control group, were abstinent. However, again there was no follow-up or use of objective, externally validated measures.

Steinglass (1979), utilizing a comprehensive battery of evaluative instruments with alcoholic families before treatment and at 6-month follow-up, found that five of nine alcoholics were drinking less at follow-up. Overall positive changes in psychiatric symptomatology were minimal. However, when the two therapists were analyzed, the directive, forceful therapist was found to be much more successful than the passive one. Steinglass also proposed that brief, intense family therapy programs may shift rigid systems but may not provide sufficient time for beneficial shifts to be permanently incorporated.

O'Farrell and Cutter (in press) evaluated behavioral marital therapy for alcoholics, comparing it to interactional couples therapy. They found that the couples in behavioral treatment showed significantly more improvement on the Locke-Wallace Marital Adjustment Test and on a videotape of their interactions which measured positive verbal, nonverbal, and problem-solving behaviors.

THE FUTURE OF FAMILY THERAPY EVALUATION

There are many variables involved in evaluating treatment that have often been neglected and must be considered in the future. These variables include patient heterogeneity, technique variability, the deleterious or beneficial aspects of other components, patient and therapist treatment goals, and therapist attributes (McCrady & Sher, 1982). All too often, an evaluation of family treatment is offered as a measure of the success or failure of "family treatment" rather than of a specific method. Obviously, all methods of family treatment are not the same. There has been significant cross-fertilization of methods; structural family therapy, for example, is a synthesis of strategic, communications, and behavioral therapies. On the other hand, family therapists also differ; for instance, psychodynamic family therapy frequently differs greatly from structural and behavioral. Thus, we can only speak of the particular method and not generalize to all family therapy. Once we have named the method, we must then realize that individual variations are so great that everyone practices any system of therapy different from anyone else. Behavioral therapies may be advantageous here because the stages of therapy are more readily defined and thus more easily taught. To unify a form of therapy into a reproducible single entity, it has to be easy to teach. Then we must evaluate whether the therapist is continuing to do what he or she has been taught. No matter how thorough the training of a therapist has been, individual differences in personality and style will always survive. Therapist variables associated with success include empathy (Moos, 1982), interpersonal functioning (Emrick, 1982), the therapist's experience with the method

(Ziegler-Driscoll, 1977), and a directive, forceful style as opposed to a passive one (Steinglass, 1979).

Perhaps the most important variable in treatment research is accurate diagnosis of the IP, including quantification of substance abuse and elimination of extraneous diagnoses using accurate diagnostic instruments such as the SADS-L (Spitzer & Endicott, 1978). The extent of substance abuse over time also needs quantification. New techniques such as the timeline follow-back interview (Emrick, 1982) can reconstruct substance-abusing behavior over a specified interval by focusing on key events and relating them to substance intake and periods of abstinence. The Addictions Severity Index (McLellan, Luborsky, Woody, & O'Brien, 1980) can also be used to quantify substance intake.

Eventually, we will also have to consider variations in the immediate family environment (the ecosystem) when we evaluate the family's baseline functioning pathology and ability to change.

Lastly, our new emphasis on the biological aspects of substance abuse must be considered as we evaluate families and treatment outcome. We should tune into subtle as well as gross manifestations of biological factors: the physical aspects of dependence and withdrawal, the acute and chronic mental syndrome, debilitating physical disease, and so on. All of these profoundly affect family function and need to be taken into account in assessing a family. We might utilize a test such as the categories subtest of the Halsted-Reitan (1955) to assess cognitive dysfunction in alcoholics and chronic drug abusers and ascertain how gradations of mental impairment in the IP affect the family. We also may look at right and left brain types of functioning in couples and how it relates to interpersonal complementary and marital satisfaction.

RECENT DEVELOPMENTS IN FAMILY
THERAPY

One issue that has generated tremendous recent interest is cybernetics and its relationship to a new epistemology. Cybernetics recently has turned from observing systems to the specific study of helping and intervention systems. Thus, this field should help us broaden our view, moving from the therapist–family holon to the reciprocal loops of supervisory group–supervisor–therapist–patient–nuclear family–family of origin–ecosystem. Cybernetics also advocates an emphasis on change rather than growth, the therapist changing along with the system, and the danger of the therapist placing him or herself above the family system (Steier, 1983).

Cybernetics is just one of the contributions to the new systems of family therapy which are presently evolving. Most of these systems involve creative, oten paradoxical strategies, which have been hypothesized to emanate from the therapist's right brain. These techniques tend to make change by unbalancing and creating crises in a family, thus forcing the family to reorganize and create a new equilibrium. These techniques have been summarized excellently by Stanton (1981), who stated that these strategic techniques have broken tremendous new ground in the development of innovative treatment models and that we can look with great anticipation and excitement to fullfillment of the promises these techniques offer. Despite my own more eclectic approach, I too find that these models bear great hope for the future. I also feel that much future promise will be found through a personal integration of many of the models described in this book, particularly as applied to more clearly defined and understood aberrant family systems.

--- REFERENCES

Cadogan, D.A. Marital group therapy in the treatment of alcoholism. *Quarterly Journal of Studies on Alcohol*, 1973, *34*, 1184–1194.
Dinaburg, D., Glick, I.D., & Feigenbaum, E. Marital therapy of women alcoholics. *Journal of Studies on Alcohol*, 1975, *36* 1245–1257.
Emrick, C. *Directions in alcohol abuse treatment research*. Newport, Rhode Island, Oct, 1982. N. Noel and LB. McCrady (Eds.). Proceedings in Press.
Hendricks, W.J. Use of multifamily counseling groups in treatment of male narcotic addicts. *International Journal of Group Psychotherapy*, 1971 *21*, 34–90.

Janzen, C. Families in the treatment of alcoholism. *Journal of Studies on Alcohol,* 1977, *38,* 114–130.

Kaufman, E. & Kaufmann, P. Multiple family therapy: A new direction in the treatment of drug abusers. *American Journal of Drug and Alcohol Abuse,* 1977 4(4), 467–478.

Meeks, D.C., & Kelly, C. Family therapy with families of recovering alcoholics. *Quarterly Journal of Studies on Alcohol,* 1970, *31,* 399–413.

Moos, R. *Directions in alcohol abuse treatment research.* Newport, Rhode Island, Oct, 1982. Proceedings in Press edited by N. Noel and B. McCrady.

Moos, R.H., Insel, P.M., & Humphrey, B. *Combined preliminary manual for family, work, and group environment scales.* Palo Alto, Calif.: Consulting Psychologists Press, 1974.

McCrady, B., & Sher, K. *Alcoholism treatment research: Treatment variables, directions in alcohol abuse treatment research,* Newport, Rhode Island: October, 1982, N. Noel and B. McCrady (Eds.). Proceedings in Press.

McLellan, A.T., Luborsky, L., Woody, G.E., & O'Brient, G.P. An improved diagnostic evaluation instrument for substance abuse patients: The addiction severity index. Journal of Nervous and Mental Disease, 1980, *168,* 26–33.

O'Farrell, T.J., & Cutter, H.S. Evaluating behavioral marital therapy for alcoholics: Procedures and preliminary results in Los Angeles. L.A. Hamerlynck (Ed.), *Essentials of behavioral treatment for families.* New York: Brunner/Mazel, in press.

Olson, D. Personal communication, 1982.

Olson, D.H. Insiders' and outsiders' views of relationships: Research studies. In G. Levinger & H. Rausch, Eds., *Close Relationships.* Amherst, Mass: University of Massachusetts Press, 1977.

Olson, D.H. Clinical rating scales for circumplex model of marital and family systems. *Family Social Science.* St. Paul, Minn.: University of Minnesota Press, 1980.

Olson, D.H., Bell, R., & Portner, J. FACES: Family Adaptability and Cohesion Evaluation Scales. *Family social science.* St. Paul, Minn.: University of Minnesota Press, 1978.

Olson, D., Bell, R., & Portner, J. *FACES II. Family social science,* St. Paul, Minn.: University of Minnesota Press, 1982.

Perosa, L., Hensen, J., & Perosa, S. Development of the structural family interaction Scale. *Family Therapy,* 1981, *8*(2) 77–90.

Reitan, R.M. An investigation of the validity of Halstead's measures of biological intelligence. *Archives of Neurology and Psychiatry,* 1955, *73,* 28–35.

Scopetta, MA., King O.E., Szapocznik, J., & Tillman, W. *Ecological structural family therapy with Cuban immigrant families.* Unpublished, 1979, as cited in Stanton, 1979.

Sieburg, E. Interpersonal confirmation: a paradigm for conceptualization and measurement. San Diego: United States International University, 1975 (Eric Document Reproducing Service. No ED 098 634).

Silver, F.C., Panepinto, W.C., Arnon, D., & Swaine, W.T. A family approach in treating the pregnant addict. In E. Senay, (Ed.), *Developments in the field of drug abuse.* Cambridge, Mass.: Shenkman, 1975.

Smilkstein, G. The family APGAR: a proposal for a family function test and its use by physicians. *The Journal of Family Practice,* 1978, *6,* 1231–1239.

Spitzer, R.L., & Endicott, J. Schedule for affective disorders and schizophrenia—Lifetime version. *Biometrics Research,* New York: State Psychiatric Institute, 1978.

Stanton, M.D. Some outcome results and aspects of structural family therapy with drug addicts, Proceedings of National Drug Abuse Conference, Cambridge, Mass., 1978.

Stanton, M.D., Family treatment approaches to drug abuse problems: A review. *Family Process,* 1979, *18,* 251–280.

Stanton, M.D. Some overlooked aspects of the family and drug abuse. In B.G. Ellis (Ed.), *Drug abuse from the family perspective.* National Institute of Drug Abuse, Department of Health, Education and Welfare, 1980.

Stanton, M.D. Strategic approaches to family therapy. In A.S. Gurman & D.P. Kniskern (Eds.), *Handbook of family therapy.* New York: Brunner/Mazel, 1981, 361–402.

Stanton, M.D., & Todd, T.C. *The family therapy of drug abuse and addiction.* New York: Guilford Press, 1982.

Steier, F. The American Society for Cybernetics: Interest group on the cybernetics of helping. *International Network of Family Therapy Newsletter,* 1983, *1*:4.

Steinglass, P. An experimental treatment program for alcoholic couples. *Journal of Studies on Alcohol,* 1979, *40,* 159–182.

Winer, LR., Lorio, J.P., & Scrofford, I. Effects of treatment on drug abusers and family. *Report to Special Action Office for Drug Abuse Prevention, 1974* as cited in Stanton, 1979.

Wunderlick, R.A., Lozes, J., & Lewis, J. Recidivism rates of group therapy participants and other adolescents processed by a juvenile court. *Psychotherapy: Theory, Research and Practice,* 1979, *11,* 243–245.

Ziegler-Driscoll, G. Family research study at Eagleville Hospital and Rehabilitation Center. *Family Process*, 1977, *61*, 175–189.

Glossary

Co-alcoholic (enabler) An individual who is emotionally overinvolved with the alcoholic and who perpetuates drinking and drinking behaviors by their interaction with the alcoholic. They are often in a no-win situation. e.g. Either their overprotection or withholding of caring may provoke alcoholic behavior.

cut-off The long term total severing of a relationship between two family members.

cybernetics The comparative study of the human brain and complex electronic computers.

disengagement Family relationships are distant. Support systems are not activated unless there is a very high level of stress and individual autonomy is highly valued at the cost of absence of intimacy and support.

doubling The therapist or other family or group member sits near the patient and expresses thoughts or feelings which are close to the surface but blocked off.

dry drunk A recovering alcoholic who has stopped drinking, but who continues to behave in an unreasonable, irrational and manipulative manner.

DSM III The official diagnostic nomenclature of the American Psychiatric Association.

empty chair technique The expression of feelings to an absent family member through directing these feelings towards an empty chair as if that person were sitting on the chair.

enmeshment Family relationships which are overly close and intense. Reactions to stress are immediate and communi-

221

cations are characterized by members interrupting and speaking for one another.

family of origin   The family in which the identified patient is born.

family structure   The invisible set of functional demands that organize interactions among family members. These structures are made up by affiliations, coalitions, boundaries and subsystems.

identified patient (index patient, I.P., IP)   That individual identified by the family as the one who needs help. For the purposes of this book, the IP is always a substance abuser.

ismorphic transactions   Use of many different interventions to change several different family behaviors all of which have the same underlying dysfunctional basis.

live supervision   When a therapy session is viewed through a one-way mirror and instructions are phoned in to shift the direction of the therapy. The supervisor may also enter the room and the therapist may join the supervisors or supervising team for a strategy conference.

mind reading   Anticipating a family member's reactions before they actually react and prejudging that they will again react as they have in the past.

nuclear family   The spouse and progeny of the identified patient. Also called family of procreation.

parental child   A child who has the role of parent in the family, often at the expense of developing peer relationships. May be a healthy situation if rules, role, responsibility and authority are defined.

polydrug abuse   Abuse and dependence on a combination of drugs and alcohol generally excluding heroin, particularly when there is no substance of choice.

pseudoindividuation   Substance abusers use drugs and alcohol to differentiate themselves from their parents but the difficulties which arise promote prolonged dependence.

psychoanalytic family therapy   A method which utilizes the individual unconscious, transference and countertransference. As used in this book, it is synonymous with psychodynamic family therapy.

retroflexing   Keeping anger inward and turning it against one's self.

slip   A return to substance abuse by a person who is a recovering alcoholic or drug abuser. For someone in A.A., any use of drugs or alcohol is considered a slip.

splitting   Two or more family members are played off against each other by a third person—leads to alienation between first two and renders them ineffective as partners.

substance abuse   The use of a psychoactive drug, alcohol, or a combination of the two to the extent that it seriously interferes with an individual's physical health, social relationships, or vocational functioning. The official diagnostic criteria are: a pattern of pathological use, impairment in social or occupational functioning due to substance use and a minimal duration of disturbance of at least one month.

substance dependence   The presence of either tolerance or withdrawal and, for a diagnosis of alcohol or marijuana dependence, a pattern of pathological use and/or social or occupational impairment.

transgenerational coalition   The overly close relationship between one parent and a child which enmeshes this child and alienates the other parent from both spouse and child.

triangulation   Conflict between two persons is displaced into a third person or issue.

Index